Dear Parents...

Micheline Mason

Dedicated to
Christopher Harrison

With very many thanks to:

Simone Aspis, Cornelia Broesskamp, Larry O Bryan, Baroness Jane Campbell DBE, Fayon Cottrell, Jackie Downer MBE, Tara Flood, Joe Gault, Mary Harrison, Alan Holdsworth (Johnny Crescendo), Haq Ismail, Luke Jackson, Maureen Johnson, Ali Kashmiri, Wilma Lawrie, John Ley, Edwina Macarthy, Maresa MacKeith, Chris O'Mahony, Rosaleen Moriarty-Simmonds, Dave Morris, Sapna Ramnani, David Ruebain, Laureen Summers, Alan Tyne and Nancy Willis, whose contributions gave such life to the words.

'Freaks, Geeks & Asperger Syndrome' by Luke Jackson reproduced by kind permission of Jessica Kingsley Publishers

Dear Parents...

Published by Inclusive Solutions 2008

ISBN: 0-9546351-5-9

Cover photo by Alan Sprung
Layout and Design by www.fivebeans.co.uk
Printed by Parker and Collinson Ltd

About the Author

Micheline was born in Surrey in 1950. She was diagnosed with Osteogenesis Imperfecta (brittle bones) at the age of four days, from which point followed a long series of hospital stays, home tuition, special schools until finally finding her freedom at the age of 17 when she joined the mainstream world by attending Croydon College of Art.

She went on to be one of the first members of the Disability Movement which grew rapidly in the UK during the late 70's and early 80's, during which time she became a Disability Equality Trainer.

At the age of 32 she became a single parent. This turned her attention to supporting the life chances of young disabled people, their parents and teachers. In 1990 she helped found the Alliance for Inclusive Education which she directed for sixteen years.

She also worked for and supported Parents for Inclusion, a 'sister' organisation, developing and delivering training courses for parents who were struggling to be good allies to their children in a very unsupportive world.

She lives in London and is now a freelance trainer, writer, artist and poet, still believing that inclusion is the key to a more rational and safe world for everyone.

Visit www.michelinemason.com

Contents

About Writing This Book

I have worked alongside non-disabled parents of disabled young people for the last 20 years, since the day I myself needed help and support to fight for the rights of my daughter within the education system. I went for advice to what was then called 'Parents in Partnership' and what is now called 'Parents for Inclusion'. I knew I needed them. I did not foresee how much they needed me.

Most parents get on the steepest "learning curve" of their lives when they have a child with a significant impairment. The close relationship with a real disabled person, their own child, may well challenge everything those parents thought they knew or understood about the world, their friends, themselves. For most, it is a lonely and painful journey because they are discovering a vicious oppression from which they now cannot hide or avoid and which they see is hurting an innocent person whom they (usually) have grown to love passionately, and who is dependent upon them for a "life".

I learned that the people who are best qualified to support those families are disabled adults, who have carved a positive life for themselves by refusing to accept the oppression. This group of people have three valuable gifts to bring families with disabled children - firstly, clarity about the real value of the child, and the existence of an oppression which distorts the truth; secondly tools to help untangle fact from fiction (developed via Disability Equality Training); and thirdly living proof that disability does not necessarily prevent a person from having a good life. This is of as much value to the child, as to the parents.

My background, apart from being a life-long disabled person, was as an activist and Disability Equality Trainer. As such I had many friends and colleagues who had also grown up as disabled children. Our collective body of experience, our hindsight and current perspective on the issue of 'disability' brought fresh insight and courage to the parents we met. They felt that they were hearing the voice of their child-grown-up and we forged a powerful alliance which has survived to this day.

I wanted to write a book which would give the same level of insight and courage to a much wider audience of parents and those who support them. To do this I invited a range of disabled people – and I am using this term as defined by the Disability Movement to include people with physical, sensory, intellectual and emotional impairments – most of whom are aged 35 or over, to offer their thinking on these two questions:

What did your parents do well to support you as a child?

What do you wish they had known, or done differently?

I chose this age group because I know that it takes a certain level of time, experience and reflection to grasp the full effects of the things which happen to us as children.

I tried also to invite contributions from as diverse a group as I could, including type and 'severity' of impairment, social class, ethnic and religious background, gender and sexual identity within the commonality of our experience of growing up with the label of 'Disabled' (or 'handicapped' as we were once called).

Because not everyone can express themselves easily through the written word, two people's contributions were gained through an assistant trained in Facilitated Communication, and two were transcriptions from interviews.

It turned out that some people I approached could not write about issues which still feel raw and unresolved. Others were too anxious that their parents would get to read what they really felt after a lifetime of hiding such feelings from them. After a lot of encouragement from me, however, contributions started to trickle into my In-Box. Some of them took my breath away.

A few pieces were taken from previously written material produced for other purposes but which illustrated certain points with great clarity.

Very few non-disabled people were invited to write, but exceptions were made for some of the members of the Circle of Support for Aaron Johnson and for his mother Maureen. The quote from 'Equal Futures' is also an exception as are the quotes from Cornelia Broesskamp and Alan Tyne.

When the first draft was complete I sent it out to all the contributors and asked for their comments, additions, alterations and final permission to publish. The end result is a unique 'mosaic' of wonderful 'patches' sewn together by myself – a quilt of joy, sadness, love, anger, and unbelievable resilience in the face of a world unready and often unwilling to welcome and accept us. I am very grateful therefore to those brave souls who have made this book a rich, vibrant, emotional, wise and hopefully empowering resource for all who read it.

When reading this book either as a parent or as someone who wants to support young disabled people and their families, please don't fill in an imaginary test paper with tick boxes to work out how well or badly you are doing. I have assumed that we have all done the best we could with the information and resources we had. If this book adds more information and resources to your store, be pleased that from now on you will be able to do even better.

Dedication

This book is dedicated to the father of my daughter, and one-time close friend, Christopher Harrison. He is unable to tell his own story, much of it remaining hidden, even from those of us who knew him well.

Chris was born blind and lived with his British born parents for the first few years of his life in Argentina. At the age of three his parents were persuaded by the RNIB (Royal National Institute for the Blind) to send him to England, to a residential 'Sunshine Home' where they promised all his special needs would be met.

He told me of the total shock and sense of abandonment he felt on the day he realised his beloved Mum was leaving him alone in a strange place where people did not even speak his native language of Spanish. He claimed he only cried that one night and then decided to stop feeling anything. His mother stayed nearby for several weeks to try and 'settle him in' and then went home to Argentina.

Academically he did well, having a sharp mind and a growing passion for politics. He was the first blind student to go to Cambridge University. He was also a very talented singer, songwriter and musician, able to play the piano and guitar from ear. He was kind and funny and deeply wished to make the world a better place, especially for young people. However, emotionally he never recovered from his early trauma or the subsequent fragmentation of his family. He found living outside of the structure of an institution very difficult. He started to endure bouts of depression in his late teens. He obtained work but found it hard to keep it. By his thirties he was a regular in-patient of psychiatric hospitals and on permanent medication. One of the side effects of the medication was that he lost the sensitivity in his fingertips and was no longer able to read Braille or play the guitar.

His unstable mental health was one of the causes of the breakdown of his first marriage to Mary, and made it difficult for him to play the part he wished in his daughter's life (we lived in the same neighbourhood).

Despite a second marriage and a ten year period of relative mental stability, he finally took his own life in 2006.

Christopher's parents were doing their best but they had been given all the wrong information and no support to keep their family together. There has never been a serious longitudinal study (a study which covers many years) into the long-term effect of the medical model on the lives of disabled children. There are only such stories, many too painful to write down or even speak about. I would like to think this book will help to make sure there are no more stories like this to be told.

Introduction

Did I Ever Thank You Dad?

Did I ever thank you Dad
For looking at me with such delight
Whilst all others were wringing their hands
Lost in the deadly imagined tragedy
Of the Brittle Bone Baby
Your sparkling green eyes alone
Sent me a life-line
A connection so brief
But strong enough to anchor me
Through those terrifying whispered half-lit hospital nights
Knowing
You would come to my rescue

Did I ever thank you Dad
For all the skills you learnt
Through gruelling apprenticeships
Employed for our comfort, security and peace
Sleeves rolled up, sawing and hammering,
Plastering and painting
Digging and planting,
Stripping down and mending
Labouring at work
Labouring at home
Seldom resting
Whistling, tired and proud

Did I ever thank you Dad
For the games, the cuddles, the jokes
For carrying me on your shoulders
Riding me on your bike

Our harmonica playing funny man
My sister and I
Rolled up with laughter
In nonsense bed time fun

Did I ever thank you Dad
For telling me that you were content
That we seemed to be enough for you
Worth all the energy you spent
You treasured us all
Though the world saw me with pity
You saw me with pride
Your artist, your thinker, your fighter
I saw never saw shame in your eyes

Your big heart gave out too soon Dad
So much success you didn't see
Grandchildren you never met
You were worn out by childhood hunger
Being a soldier in an unwanted war
Three jobs to make ends meet
A fireman hero rushing into danger
When all others are rushing out
Always being brave
Always being
A man.

Micheline Mason 2006

The strongest bond between human beings is the bond between parents and their children. We are designed that way. A child is a fully formed person. In order to remain that person, and to develop, we need to be touched, loved, fed and kept warm. We need a safe environment and lots of stimulation for our brains to develop. We need this for a long time. In fact we need it throughout our lives because we continue to develop until the day we die.

We come into the world expecting one or more people to be waiting for us, willing and ready to answer these needs. With our parents support we usually manage to survive all manner of challenges and difficulties, becoming equipped to take our place in our communities, make our own contributions and love others.

If we do not receive that support we do not do well. We feel alone and abandoned. The drive to get our needs met becomes an overriding occupation. We do not learn as well, our behaviour is altered, and sometimes we just give up.

For all parents this is a daunting job, but if your child is seriously ill, disabled, or seemingly not following the expected path of development, then you are also going to have to deal with some mighty forces in society which may confuse you, making your job more difficult and make you feel very alone.

The majority of parents in this position have not experienced the same struggles as their child. They may never have had meaningful relationships with disabled people and will be relying for help and advice from professionals who, in reality, know little about the real lives of disabled people. Parents are, therefore, deprived of vital information which could help them steer a clearer path through life for their child and their family.

This book is an attempt to fill that gap to bring the experience of those of us who were once those children growing up with parents just like you. We want to reach out and remind you of the fundamental importance of your relationship with your child. We want to tell you what our parents did well, usually using pure instinct, so you can draw confidence when your instincts say the same things. We want also to tell you of times our parents did not know enough, were pulled off course by misguided advisers, or became embroiled in the wrong battles. We want to tell you this so you do not exhaust yourselves unnecessarily, or find you and your son or daughter has arrived at an unwanted destination. Mostly we are telling you this so you can get a different perspective, or viewpoint, on the task ahead of you which will hopefully become more joyful and fulfilling. You will be learning how to become 'allies' to disabled and other 'labelled' peoples. This is not necessarily an easy road to take, but just by being on it you will become someone who helped change the world.

The Importance of a Welcome

For most human beings being born is the time of our lives when people are really excited about us. They have been waiting and planning, creating a space for us to fill. We arrive naked and needy, unable to do anything for ourselves and everyone around us is just thrilled. Everyone wants to see us, touch us, hold us, explore all our little bits, pass us round to be admired. We get cards and presents. Maybe new toys are bought, and most importantly, our Mum cradles us for hours, feeding us and looking at us and talking to us in a special Mummy voice. Hopefully, there is Daddy too, maybe Nanny, Aunties and Uncles, sisters and brothers, a whole community into which we fit and belong. For a while at least our needs are allowed to shape the responses and routines of our people. We learn that we matter. We are welcomed. Even if life is downhill after that, the fact that our first experiences were positive lays an emotional foundation for everything that follows. The right neural pathways are laid down and our brain chemistry is correctly balanced. We are all set to become a fully rounded human being, able to develop freely and take on life to the full.

This welcome goes beyond the immediate family. All societies know that they need new people to survive and progress. Birth rituals and celebrations are held amongst all the cultures of the world.

If, however, the baby is born with difficulty, may appear to be not well, or to have some impairment then this welcome quickly fades. Voices go quiet. Curtains are drawn around the mother's bed. People do not send the card they bought or make the phone call they had planned. Visitors stay away, or came and say they are 'sorry'. The medical profession go into overdrive. Of course, if this means saving a child's life, it is not a bad thing in itself. In fact it is a wonderful thing for those of us who have access to so many resources, but so often these first responses are laden with negativity and fear, outdated attitudes and misinformation. Even when a condition is not life threatening, doctors often feel they have to spell out everything they think is wrong with the child, all their symptoms and possible treatments. Sometimes they make sweeping statements about the likely future of the child leaving the parents full of anxiety and fear.

David describes his 'welcome':

"My earliest memory of those around me was of anxiety and even terror, on account of being noticeably, physically disabled. Many, if not most, people looked scared or pitiful and treated me accordingly. I am told that, when I was born, there was a discussion at the hospital as to whether my parents should "leave" me there (I was not ill in any way). I recall great confusion and then terror on my part that I was not good enough, and that I had to compensate others for my physical "flaws". The damage caused to me was profound and lasting and it was not until later on in adulthood that I understood that it need not have been that way. I am sure that joyous, tender love was all that was required."
David Ruebain

The baby, or child, is met with a very different response to other babies, not just from his or her parents or family, but from the wider world around them. The Welcome suddenly seems conditional on something they could not possibly understand. They are a disappointment. They are a worry. There is something wrong with them but they do not know what it is or how to put it right.

One danger is that this response may interfere with the natural bond between parents and their children. Anger, fear, guilt, shame may replace the delight, the pride and the hope that the parents once had. The child may start to feel insecure, afraid. They may appear distressed and no one will know if this distress is related to 'what is wrong with them' or something else, adding to the confusion and anxiety of the adults around them.

Some doctors and medical professionals, fearing a negative response from parents, will sometimes hold off telling them that their child may have an impairment even though they have suspicions. The parents may then have to fight for recognition of their child's difficulties. This is also not helpful.

All babies need and deserve a big welcome whatever struggles they may have ahead. No one can prophecy the future of any child, and no parent needs to be made to feel their child is less valuable than others. Jackie is clear what she thinks should happen:

"I think doctors and other professionals need lots more training in how to talk to parents and disabled people – not to be so negative. If you have a disabled baby you can be happy about it."
Jackie Downer MBE

Bring out the champagne. Take photos. Celebrate.

Diagnosis

The World Stepped Back

Once I was an ordinary baby
Chubby arms
Tiny fingernails
A shock of hair
Someone to be loved
Cuddled and sung to
Bathed and fed
Close to my mother
A bright future ahead
I felt safe

I was an ordinary baby
For four short days
Before the cold table
The huge camera
The radiographer's skill
Revealed my hidden secret
And the world stepped back
Abandoning me
To forces we could not fight
Larger than love
Judgement
A redefining of my value
A bleak future
All delight snuffed out
Like a light

What could I make of this?
Left to scream
In my hospital cot
I felt irredeemably flawed
Flailing in space
My future in doubt

My Daddy's eyes saved me
Green and sparkly
The delight came back
As we looked and looked
The connection once made
Could not be broken
The look reminded me
I had once felt safe
And I knew,
Somehow I knew
He would come back one day
Not just to visit
But to take me home

Micheline December 2007

Diagnosis is a crucial issue, especially for children. One the one hand, because of the social context of being identified as a disabled person the point of diagnosis can be traumatic - the point of total re-evaluation of the child's worth, a sort of instant down grading which can have enormous impact of their sense of 'welcome', value or even safety in the world. Chris recalls the time when her deafness was first diagnosed:

" No one was aware of my impairment until a school nurse diagnosed it at 7. I was probably born deaf in one ear but there is some confusion about this. My paternal grandmother was deaf and it is likely I inherited the condition. Until I was 11 or so, I was only deaf in one ear and so could 'get by' fairly well.

However, at the point of diagnosis, it seemed the world went mad. I was ferried to and from Great Ormond Street dozens of times and had some hideous and uncomfortable outpatient and inpatient treatments inflicted upon me (for instance having liquid forced up my nose under pressure, or having my ear drum perforated.) whilst my parents sat by smiling and thanking the consultant for his attention".
Chris O'Mahony

Some parents are aware of what they may call the 'stigma' of disability and avoid naming it, talking about it or giving their child information about their impairment, as if doing so would avoid the stigma. Chris goes on to explain the difficulties this can cause:

"No one ever explained to me why I was deaf, what the treatments were supposed to accomplish, or why I was in hospital. No-one ever asked me how I felt or what I thought about it all.

It had a bad effect on my relationship with my parents, who never discussed my deafness with me. They simply told me to sit near the front of the class and pay attention. I know they worried, but this did not translate into any positive support for me.

I struggled with school, partly because my mother had a horror of hearing aids. I would hear lots of 'funny' stories about my grandmother and her hearing aid and it didn't take much to persuade me that I didn't want 'one of those things on your chest' (as my mother described it to me). However, I was very successful at primary school because I am a natural lip-reader. Once at secondary school, everything changed as teachers spoke to the class with their backs to us whilst writing on the board. I missed whole chunks of narrative and began to think I was stupid because I didn't know the lessons.

At home, my parents just nagged me about my schoolwork. They never asked if I was struggling and I was never allowed to use my deafness as an excuse. In fact, it never occurred to me to use my deafness as an excuse. I was obviously stupid and the only way to cover it up was to misbehave and be funny and popular – I was good at that! I eventually left school with no qualifications having spent almost a whole term playing truant. This was a secret grief to me at the time because I did love to learn things but just couldn't seem to do it in a classroom setting".
Chris O' Mahony

The 'stigma' attached to disability needs to be traced back to its historical roots, thoroughly examined in a critical sense, and exposed as the myth or stereotyping it generally is, based on false information which has been replaced over time with actual facts. Religion has played its part too, or rather the distortion of religious beliefs by superstition and oppression. All this needs to be separated from straight biological information which is neutral, and often very useful and interesting.

For you to fully support your child, it is necessary that you get good information yourself. Rosaleen reminds us that we need to find out things from many different sources to get a complete picture:

"The moment you know that you are carrying a disabled child, or once you have given birth and discovered that your child is disabled, or if your child becomes disabled in later life - ask questions about the impairment (medical condition) that your child now has. Speak to other parents with children in a similar situation. Speak to other people with the same impairment. And of course the medical profession can give you their point of view as well. Don't be afraid to ask probing questions, most people when they understand why you need to know certain things, will be happy to answer your questions as honestly as they can."
Rosaleen Moriarty- Simmons

One reason to look for information from many sources is that the medical profession do not know everything. Sometime, their diagnoses are wrong. Haq tells the harrowing story of the misdiagnosis which led to his impairment becoming much more significant than necessary:

"I began to lose my sight when I was about 11, but no one knew what was going on. At school I had to keep asking where the line was to write. My writing had gone wonky. People shouted at me because they didn't understand. My brother got angry and my parents seemed aloof. I had severe headaches. I was always in pain. I went backwards and forwards to hospital, I remember giving myself eye tests, standing at the back of the living room to see what I could see. People came with their potions and remedies. They took me to different temples and prayed over me. They thought it was a brain tumour. Eventually I was sent to Barts (St. Bartholomews Hospital). I could barely see by then.

They told me they were going to put me to sleep so they could put in some eye drops, but actually they were draining fluid from my brain because of hydrocephalus. I had to have a shunt inserted into my head. I woke up before the operation was over so they had to give me more anaesthetic. They over-anaesthetised me and I had hallucinations for two days afterwards. I thought my brother had been killed and I saw war scenes that were so vivid they gave me nightmares I can still recall. I didn't know what had happened to me. I was still in pain. They said that if I had been correctly diagnosed and treated earlier, I would not have lost my sight, but by then permanent damage had been done. But I have got used to managing with the little sight I have".
Haq Ismail.

Mary and her brother Phillip were also given a false picture of their impairments:

"The medical advice about our condition was pretty gloomy and, as it turned out, completely wrong due to a complete misdiagnosis. We were not expected to live past our 20's."
Mary Harrison

More often, their prognoses are wrong. A prognosis should be an educated guess as to the development of an impairment over time, but it is common for doctors to share with you their opinions and fears for the future based on a small number of case histories, as if it were inevitable.

When my impairment (brittle bones) was diagnosed my parents were told that I would die within a few months. When I didn't, they told them I would never be able to live a normal life and could not even be hugged or cuddled. I am glad to say none of this was true.

John tells of his mother's confession:

"My Mum had a habit of telling me the truth, even if it was not what I needed to hear. She told me how she had read my medical notes which prophesised that I would be "Confined to wheelchair and totally dependant on others

always!" Apparently this news sent her into a coma for 2 days".
John Ley

Rosaleen describes her early years:

"I was born disabled with foreshortened arms and legs caused by the drug Thalidomide. At the time the medical profession held out few expectations for my life. It may sound like a cliché but they actually said things like "she will remain a cabbage for the rest of her life, stuck laying on her back unable to do anything". How proud am I to have been able to prove them wrong."
Rosaleen Moriarty-Simmonds

A New Route

Why is it so difficult for disabled people to be valued as equals? In the last 30 years or so, around the world, disabled people have been coming together to try and shed some light on these issues and to try to guide people along a path which is rational and life-enhancing and away from old myths, misguided policies, half truths and fear. We have called the old route the 'Medical Model' and the new route the 'Social Model'.

The Medical Model
The medical model puts the cause of our difficulties in us and our bodies.

The medical model does not mean that all medical intervention is wrong. Medicine saves lives, can restore functioning, lessen pain and even sometimes cure illnesses or impairments. Many people in the poor world are desperate for better health care. A good example of this is the comparative situation of children born with cleft palates and hare-lips. In poor countries, like the Philippines, these impairments cause life long disfigurements, and difficulties with eating and speaking. They totally dictate the life chances of the people who have them. In the rich world however such impairments are now skilfully dealt with surgically in infancy leaving very little, if any, impairments or difficulties. They have become a non-issue.

Science and medicine has also helped us start to emerge from the beliefs of the 'Dark Ages' of myth and superstition. Such false beliefs still linger in many cultures around the world, attributing impairments to retribution from the Gods for past sins, the parents consorting with the Devil and so on. Bringing some objective facts into the picture has been a progressive thing, of which we need lots more. Disabled people are not arguing about this kind of useful medical intervention. The problem is when medicine is used to try and cure the incurable, solve social problems, or is used for purposes of economic or social control.

Underlying the 'medical model' are the values of the most powerful classes of people i.e. that our worth as human beings is only in our capacity

27

to be economically productive. To this end the medical model has been used to give pseudo scientific justification to many policies based entirely on racism, classism and sexism used to exploit the poor. All have used notions of smaller brains, genetic weakness, inherited feeble-mindedness and undeveloped morals, as 'medical facts' when persuading people to accept slavery, workhouses, the oppression of women and the notorious eugenic policies of the 19th century which eventually led to Hitler's 'Final Solution'.

How this affects you if you yourself, or your child, is disabled, is that it views disabled people as non-productive, expensive and burdensome. It channels the majority of the resources allocated to 'disability' into medical interventions and research aimed at lowering the number of disabled children getting born through free pre-natal screening programmes, and programmes of treatment or therapy aimed at cure, or at least the ability to function without extra help. This is seen as economically prudent.

Secondly it distracts us from the major social causes of impairment such as poverty and war by medicalising the symptoms, making us think they are all caused by illness and disease, curable by pills rather than social justice and equality. One example of this is the enormous rise in the number of children being prescribed Ritalin or other powerful drugs to dampen down their energy and help them to concentrate on their schoolwork. Another is the number of adults diagnosed with 'depression', usually following bereavements, family breakdown or increasing stress at work, and treated with mind-altering drugs rather than improving the circumstances of the person's life. The mental health system medicalises our sense of injustice and the emotions which go with it, such as anger and sadness, making us think we are weak, or mad.

Thirdly, it gives the medical profession unprecedented power over our lives as they are increasingly given the role of gatekeepers to the resources we need such as benefits and allowances. Until very recently they had almost total power to decide where a disabled child should be educated regardless of the child's or the parent's wishes. Disabled adults still face institutionalisation if their care needs cost over a certain amount, all decided by medical assessments. Entitlement to aids and adaptations, or assistive technology lies in the pens of physiotherapists, speech therapists and occupational therapists who have to sign those forms. Disabled people often have to have the signed authorisation of a doctor to take part in ordinary activities such as swimming or flying in an aeroplane. Doctors, psychiatrists and psychologists are themselves torn by being expected to make recommendations based on economic factors rather than clinical need.

Fourthly, it deflects resources, both human and financial, from developing real solutions to our difficulties such as creating accessible environments or services. Even in the UK, one of the richest nations in the world, disabled children who need specialised powered wheelchairs still have to go cap-in-hand to charities to provide them.

Lastly, it makes both disabled and non-disabled people feel that people with impairments are faulty, of less worth than 'normal' people and will only ever be truly loved, valued and respected if they are able to get better, at least enough to be independent (not need help), and to work, or be productive in an unchanged able-bodied world. It focuses all attention on getting rid of the impairment rather than developing the whole person, or building inclusive communities, and in so doing causes much more real suffering than the impairment itself. It also seems to be able to stop non-disabled people from thinking rationally about us.

The Social Model
The 'social model' starts from a different place. Young disabled people living in long stay residential homes began to organise by a secret newsletter, forming 'underground' networks until they became sufficiently united to become public. The first national organisation of disabled people was UPIAS (the Union of the Physically Impaired Against Segregation) in 1972. From this body of thinkers came the beginnings of the social model of disability which firmly put the causes of our difficulties in society, its values and social systems.

Because the model was created by disabled people who had failed to become non-disabled people despite all sorts of treatments and therapies, it started by recognising their inherent worth as human beings. It acknowledges that there will always be people with impairments in the world, but these impairments do not have to prevent them from living good and meaningful lives if the communities in which they live are welcoming, and designed to accommodate their needs. People who created this new viewpoint had suffered, not from the impairments themselves, but from the imposition of a system which separated them from their families and local communities, sheltered them from ordinary life, imposed on them their own impossible goals whilst ignoring their own, and made them feel deeply ashamed of themselves and each other.

The social model sees disabled people as a large minority group whose rights have been denied through attitudinal, social, physical and legal barriers within society. It separates the impairment, or medical condition, from the effects of these barriers which disabled them, but which can be removed by planned social action. After many years of struggle, this new model is gradually being adopted by mainstream society and its services.

The medical model has shaped our past. Hopefully the social model will shape our future. We are all struggling within a period of transition from one to the other and this means that you, as parents, almost daily have to use your judgement to choose between two different sets of options, some of which are cleverly disguised. No one can pretend this is easy.

As we look at some of the main issues before you, you will see how these contrary views will be a challenge in everything in your families life from how your child is welcomed into the world, how your wider family react to the news, how professionals approach you, what help is on offer, where your children are directed for their education, what legal rights your child has, what opportunities there are for inclusion within their communities, even what dreams and aspirations they are allowed to have. It cannot be avoided but it can at least be explained and challenged.

The Medical Model and the Breaking of Relationships

"I was born in 1956. I had cerebral palsy. My mother could not cope with this idea and, after one year, she left us. My Dad looked after me with the help of my grandparents. When I was about 5 my Dad married again.
Edwina Macarthy

It is still a fact that many parents abort their unborn children if they are told they are 'defective', and are encouraged to abandon their living disabled children, even here in the so called 'Developed World'.

"My parents were very young when I was born and virtually everybody around them said, "leave your child here [hospital], go away and start your life all over again". One day, probably having been deluged with such advice or perhaps at their lowest ebb, my parents did take me to the gates of the local orphanage. I tell you with huge relief and great admiration that they turned around took me back home and never again considered doing anything other than bringing me up as their firstborn, and much loved daughter."
Rosaleen Moriarty-Simmonds

Even if it doesn't happen (or nearly happen) to us, we are painfully aware that it may have happened to our friends, and are full of fear that it could be us one day in the future. Tara speaks of her fear of being anything less than a model child in case her parents completely abandoned her at boarding school:

"I remember being extremely homesick during this period of my life, but chose not to tell my parents what was going on because I didn't want to cause any trouble. I had seen other children arriving at Chailey with their parents and then never seeing their families again. There were loads of children whose parents had abandoned them. I was terrified of the same thing happening to me so I did everything I could when I was at home to be everything I thought my parents wanted me to be. I was very well behaved – unnaturally so."
Tara Flood

Edwina, who was sent to the same school, tells of similar feelings, including the sense that she could not tell her family how she felt:

"I felt hurt to be sent away. It was like losing my mum again. But I was lucky - my parents came down every week. Some people were left. Some didn't even go home for school holidays. I didn't tell them how I felt. Even now I hate Sundays because that's the day people leave me."
Edwina Macarthy

Our natural instincts as human beings are always in favour of life. We want to live our own life well. We want to connect to other people. We want to help other people to have a good life, especially our children. When we think our child is in danger, we want to protect them. But if this is true, why do we do such horrible things to innocent children?

Many people, including me, have noticed that people have to believe that whatever they are doing is right, justifiable and for the greater good, before they can do it. Hitler, Stalin, Saddam all believed passionately in the correctness of what they were doing, as did many of their followers. Many deeply religious people have gone to war believing they have God on their side, and many disabled people have been treated with the utmost cruelty whilst the people doing it believed they were being kind.

Ever since I was a small child I have wondered why this is, how it happens - what is done to non-disabled people that they have such good intentions and yet get it so wrong? I don't know the complete answer to that yet, but I have noticed a few things.

The medical model, until very recently, dominated all the air space – books, training courses, television, radio, advertising, fund raising, journalism – everything. It was all created by non-disabled people, mostly those with professional status. At the same time, unless you were disabled yourself or had a close family member who was disabled, you probably did not ever meet disabled people other than as 'clients' or patients, or saw them in large groups looking and sounding odd and being bussed somewhere apart and different. Consequently you had no real information about the reality of disabled people's lives and, in that vacuum, you were easily led to believe a whole lot of things which were not true. You were given a false picture of reality and that picture was frightening and uncomfortable and one most people would rather not think about. The medical model has persuaded people that disabled people are different to them, need different things and don't have the same feelings as 'normal' people. It has portrayed us as all child-like, not able to know what is best for us. It has kept people focussed on our difficulties and deficits so it is easy to think we are useless, burdensome and dispensable.

Remembering that the roots of this model lie in a very murky past, it is possible to see a sort of dark logic to it all. If the wealthy elite believe that disabled people will reduce the profits they can make by being unproductive and needy, and that the parents of disabled children will want to keep them, love them and protect them so they can live a whole, expensive, lifetime, then it makes sense to try and stop this love from ever starting in the first place.

This thinking is clear when we look at our state funding of a national pre-natal screening programme coupled with differential abortion laws. These disallow the termination of non-disabled foetuses after 24 weeks (when it is expected that the child could live independently of her/his mother) whilst allowing the termination of disabled foetuses up to full term. All the State now has to do is persuade the parents that killing their child is a kind thing to do. This is done by the perpetual emphasis on our difficulties, deficits and suffering whilst clamping a big metaphorical hand over the mouths of disabled people. All this seems to result in non-disabled people having their warm natural responses shut down. I believe it has caused a kind of psychic wound on society as a whole, interfering with our thinking and ability to make proper links between cause and effect.

Wounds however can be healed. If you are reading this book you are already starting the process. The following chapters look at the different stages of parenting and some of the common issues which are likely to arise. Each one looks at the dangers and at some of the possible ways to avoid them, or create a new response to them which will help your child to develop their true selves.

The Child's Experience of The Medical Model

Get Better for Mummy

Won't you smile for Mummy
Won't you smile and look at me
Won't you look at me and say a word
Just say a word or two
Won't you speak to me and smile
Won't you sit up please
Won't you sit up and smile and speak to me
Won't you ever walk
Won't you stand up and smile and speak to me
Won't you read and write
Won't you do your sums and pass your tests
Won't you stand up and smile and talk and walk and read and write and
pass your tests
For Mummy and Daddy who love you
And don't want you to be tossed away
With the other garbage
Won't you just get better for Mummy and Daddy
So we know we haven't failed you?

Won't you smile at me Mummy
Won't you touch my face and know I can feel you
Won't you listen to me Mummy
Speaking without words
Won't you notice that I am happy
Happy when you smile and touch me
Won't you help me to sit up
With soft plump pillows
Won't you lend me your arms and legs
To help me explore the world
Seeking the joy of friendship
Won't you tell the teachers

That words on paper are not the only way
To share our gifts
Won't you tell me you love me Mummy
In all my imperfection
Won't you tell the world Mummy
That human beings do not belong on garbage heaps
But in close communities of learning
Where we all struggle together
Won't you be proud of me Mummy and Daddy
Just the way I am
So I know I haven't failed you?

Micheline Mason March 2005

Disabled children, especially those of us born with our impairments, experience the world as a very strange place. We start off feeling fine about ourselves! We feel we are just as we should be. We come into the world expecting to find a joyous welcome by warm, loving human beings who will use their intelligence to keep us safe, and meet our needs. Instead we are met with what often feels like a sort of madness. People around us are acting as though something is terribly wrong and gradually it dawns on us that we are somehow causing all this pain and anxiety, but we don't know why. Dave recounts:

"I think that me and my mother spent a lot of preschool time trying to answer the question everybody was asking as my development did not meet expectations. "What is wrong with him?" I don't ever remember feeling wrong, but it was clearly important, so we went to doctors and clinics to find out what sort of wrong I was.

We started with local doctors who tended to scratch their chins when my reflexes did not conform to their expectations when they hit my knees and elbows with their hammers and creased my feet with their sharp pointers. We visited The Bobath clinic in St John's Wood. We visited bone specialists. I was prodded and poked, samples were collected, x-

rays taken, measurements made. I learned to take the injections and other interventions with that patient dignity that comes from repetition and experience. I absorbed the acrid smell of sterility. I learned a bedside manner to engage with the physicians and preserve myself as they desperately tried to categorise my wrongness. I tried to tell them that the hammer and electric shocks would not work. Sometimes I hurt.

They eventually found out what was wrong with me at Great Ormond Street hospital by cutting out some muscle. I found out a number of things:

- walking was something I would not be doing for much longer. The last time I remember walking was across the children's ward; staggering from bed to bed playing out some scene from a John Wayne film. I remember falling exhausted not being able to get up;

- that the pain of separation hurts far more than needles. I vividly remember looking down into the courtyard of the hospital as my mother left each day for two weeks. 'Yesterday' always seemed to me playing on the radio somewhere and I can never now listen to this song without a feeling of desolation filtering into my consciousness;

-what conglomeration meant. Its definition was on the first page of Chitty Chitty Bang Bang, the book which my mother read to me in hospital. It was some sort of talisman for me as I felt scared and alone. I think I wanted to fly away in a magical car, but did not quite believe in magic.

It was finally discovered that my wrongness was genetic and 'unrightable' and not something that I would grow out of. A number of things then happened.

Firstly I became a minor curiosity in a medical sense. Another snapshot memory. Naked and alone, student doctors all around desperate to see my tongue and its constant involuntary movement. More tests. A researcher from New Zealand collected my urine for months and we stored it under the sink. My parents filled in questionnaires asking whether there was anything different or strange about my birth. I found out that I had been bathed in oil when I was born.

Secondly I somehow changed my constitution from flesh and blood to some sort of delicate breakable compound that would wither away, disappear, die. It seemed that people looked at me differently and I refused to go into restaurants because people stared. People lowered voices when they were talking about me, but I could hear their explanations and I understood very well. It's like muscular dystrophy doctors said, but nobody heard 'It's like'.

Thirdly, I was sent away."
Dave Morris

We notice many adults being drawn to poke, prod, test, and measure us. What are they trying to find? Our parents don't stop them. Indeed they encourage them. Why?

Often these adults do horrible and painful things to us in scary places called hospitals. You notice that these adults seem more powerful than your parents. You begin to wonder who 'owns' you, who has responsibility for you, is it the people who love you, or the people who definitely don't? This starts to make you feel very insecure.

You work out that something is expected of you to stop the anxiety and bring the love and joy you crave. You have to Get Better so you try and try to do the things you find the most difficult. Sometimes you succeed, much to everyone's relief. Sometimes you don't, much to everyone's disappointment and even anger. Your own interests, passions, goals are not sought out or developed. In fact there is little recognition that you might have any. And of course if this continues throughout your childhood, you will not necessarily hold on to them, often becoming very passive, even as an adult.

It is assumed you want to be 'normal' and almost any means will justify these ends. It is not so. We already feel normal. We know no other 'self'. Being us is not the same as having once been a non-disabled person who then loses some abilities. That is a different experience – one of loss and adjustment – our experience is of being whole and complete, and also unique. For any of us the attempts to change us are like having a precious part of us cut away, or discarded.

Touch, Our First Language

When I was born my bones broke like glass, but no one knew, so being born caused me much pain. Clumsy but well-meaning people pulled me out of my mother and maybe slapped me to start me breathing. Two broken legs, a slap, but still I knew I was loved. I knew because I was given to my delighted parents who saw only my shock of red hair, my tiny nails, my button nose, all those things that parents wonder over each time the miracle of life occurs. They showed me their delight by holding me close, stroking my face, letting me grasp their fingers, smiling at me with joy on their faces

I must have been in great discomfort, but still I felt safe as I was taken home to be shown off to my older sister waiting for her new playmate. Pain made me want to stay still and not be moved. I screamed each time I was lifted or nappies were changed. After four days of this my parent's anxiety took them and me back to hospital. X-rays, a diagnosis, and everything in my short life changed.

I can still feel the withdrawal of the world from me. The stepping back. Grief replaced delight, fear replaced intelligence. The white-coated professionals seem to take ownership of me on behalf of the State. I was placed in a cot. My parents were sent home. Nurses were instructed not to handle me for fear of causing further injuries to my bones. They did not consider injuries to my heart, my soul.

Touch is our first language. Strong hands are made to hold their own infants. Warm bodies meant to provide safety. Soft breasts meant to provide sustenance. All else is distant – sounds, sights; our newborn brains still have to learn to make sense of them, but touch we already know. Its comfort is instant. From that solid foundation we start to piece together the information flooding in from our other senses. We learn where we end and the world begins. We learn who is there for us. We learn where we fit in. We can learn to survive hunger, pain and fear without long-lasting damage, if held in a healing embrace.

What did I learn lying all alone in my cot, in the false safety created by my isolation? Something had gone terribly wrong and I had to be punished. Everything I needed was taken away. Warmth, closeness, love, the sensation of skin upon skin. The world had stopped communicating with me.

I can remember only darkness and a sense of danger. My physical pain I could no longer locate as coming from within. It seemed to flood me from the outside as soon as I moved with no holding restraint. My cries brought nothing but anger from overwrought staff. I learnt to keep quiet. That was the only way to survive. Still and quiet was safe. A habit of a lifetime was set in"
Micheline Mason*

Human beings need to be touched, not only when we are small babies, but all through our lives. It is a rational need. My early deprivation has only partially healed, and the healing has occurred through human contact. Living at home with little technological support, I had to be carried everywhere. I loved it. My best memories were of riding on my Dads' shoulders, or tucked on his arm as we went off to the library, or the shops, or to the swings.

There are many kinds of touch - stroking, caressing, massaging, washing, drying, hugging, carrying, wrestling, a whole language of which we are barely aware. I remember when I had my own daughter and she, having the same impairment as myself, also suffered the unavoidable pain of broken bones. For the first few years she was not hospitalised. Instead of any medical intervention she demanded a warm hand placed firmly over the part of her body which had been injured. With this touch she was visibly able to relax and to sleep the healing sleep she needed. The hand had to remain in place all day and all night. The instant I thought I would try and move she would go tense and her wail would start. We had to recruit and train volunteers to share this vigil from our circle of close friends. I was surprised at how many seemed to instinctively understand why this was so important. As a result my daughter has never learnt to connect pain with

* From 'Touch Our First Language' first published in Present Time, Rational Island Press 2005

isolation and fear, and our friends have learned how their hands can help a child to heal. Her recoveries were always remarkably fast.

Disabled children as always are at the sharp edge of life. Although my story may seem extreme, and certainly conditions for children in hospital have changed quite dramatically over the last twenty years, many disabled children still suffer from the loss of physical closeness from others. The impairments themselves, if they reduce the child's ability to move independently, may make initiating physical contact difficult, or impossible. Any contact will have to be initiated by the 'other', if at all. *(Take a moment to imagine what this would mean in your life now.)*

Disabled children may be subjected to physical touch, which is unpleasant or painful, such as the stretching exercises common in physiotherapy, or all the medical interventions involved in surgery. The memory of these experiences can leave fear and confusion which get in the way of welcoming any kind of physical closeness.

Children with high-level support needs may have these met by several different people, none of whom love the child and none of who have been chosen by the child. This is very different to having those intimate tasks done by someone who is trusted by the child – someone who is part of their emotional life. And when this all happens out of sight, in separate isolated and segregated settings, the potential for abuse becomes very real. Just as for all children in 'Care', institutional life is never safe.

'Moving and Handling'
When my daughter was growing up, I couldn't lift her myself. I had to teach many people how to lift her, and she became a true expert at this herself from a very young age. With the added complication of brittle bones, her safety depended upon it. We both learned that there are people who cannot lift because of their own impairments, and people who cannot be trusted to lift because they did not know how to listen to a child's instructions. But we also learned that most people are only too willing to be useful in this way. Some even went to gyms to strengthen their bodies

so they could manage the very precise lifts that had to be done when she had a fracture. I was surprised at how many people had to be taught how to lift safely, without hurting their backs, and how little thought they had ever given the subject. How great it would have been if lifting was considered a necessary life-skill, taught at school alongside first aid and cooking. How much better even, if people were taught how important it could be to carry a child out into the world, or into your own living room.

The long-term effects of the loss of giving or receiving human touch can affect your mind forever. We need to start to think about reclaiming the language of touch, and reclaiming our bodies as the wonderful resource they can be to each other as we struggle to be fully human. Ali describes the importance of his relationship with his Auntie:

"I did get physical contact as a child, but not from my parents. When my mum left my dad was in the habit of palming me off. He invited an Auntie from Pakistan to come and live with us to look after me. She was my saviour. She saw me for the person I was. She had insight into the oppression and the skills I would need to overcome it. She said, "Don't let anyone push you around" and I have never forgotten .She cuddled me and I sort of hid behind her. She was everything to me – mother, sister, and best friend. She gave me determination. She taught me to think for myself. She could show me her love, unlike my parents and so she gave me the ability to love."
Ali Kashmiri

Getting Help

"My parents both came from working class families to whom handouts and 'welfare' were looked on with disdain and with the attitude that if you needed help you must have mismanaged or been feckless in some way. My mother especially came from austere Scottish pillars of the Kirk stock. Working class people could be very hard on each other with the 'even though we're both poor, I'm better than you because I manage without welfare' attitude. The consequence of this belief meant that as my brother and I were growing up it was not the done thing to ask for help from people outside of the family, even though the situation was unusual in that they had two disabled children. My parents would struggle on coping with our needs even though they both had full time demanding jobs. They never actively asked for any help from 'the authorities' (and no doubt they are still proud of this). I suppose it harks back to the dreaded Victorian workhouse when families were forcibly separated and never saw each other again.

Our family house wasn't really suitable for wheelchair users. The downstairs loo was outside and impossible to get to with a wheelchair and the bedrooms and bath were upstairs. I was able to walk until I was about 15 and would crawl upstairs to bed. Dad had to carry Phil up to bed each night. As he grew up and Dad found it too much of a struggle, it was Phil who contacted social services with a view to having a downstairs bedroom and bathroom built. I wish my parents had addressed these problems earlier. I wish they'd asked to be re-housed in more accessible accommodation which would have enabled Phil to be more independent and mobile in his own right. My parents just sort of muddled through making the best of things instead of facing the difficulties head-on which would have made a difference to our life and theirs. I wish they'd known that it is OK to ask for help, that there is no shame in not being able to cope unassisted. My brother and I went on to unconsciously adopt the same attitude of not being very good at asking for the help that we needed (which in the latter stage of his life was quite considerable). It's a constant struggle even now to get the right help that we need as disabled people and you have to pull on superhuman reserves sometimes to deal with the authorities that have the power to say yea or nay, and parents and disabled

people have to learn not to take 'no' for an answer."
Mary Harrison

It is not a failure on your part to need help as a parent. Most parents could do with more help than they get. There are also a lot of things to which you and your child are entitled, some of which have been fought for very hard by disabled people and by families like yours. You could say you owe it to them to find out what they are and to go and get them. They include benefits, allowances, Direct Payments and Personal Budgets, all of which help to ease the financial situation; Toy Libraries; grants for special equipment and adaptations to you home; the possibility of a loaned car and driving lessons if your child's impairment makes it difficult to use public transport; help with holidays and support for your child to access local activities; the assessment and meeting of your child's 'Special Educational Needs'; support groups; shared-care schemes and training courses.

If you are disabled yourself, you are entitled to resources such as Direct Payments in order to help you carryout your responsibilities as a parent. Disabled parents are particularly afraid to appear unable to cope and may struggle unnecessarily without support. Many of us fear that it may lead to us being labelled as incapable and our children being taken into care. Don't let this unlikely fear stop you. Get advice from a specialist organisation such as the Disabled Parents Network*.

The best place to find out about all these things are from disabled people, other families, local advice centres; local Centres for Independent Living, relevant charities or pressure groups and of course the Internet. Do not wait for the statutory services to tell you your rights – you might be waiting a long time! The information pages at the back of this book may be a good starting point.

I think it is safe to say that the process of getting these things may well drive you bonkers, and will require you to plumb the depths of your patience and persistence.

* See 'Useful Organisations' at the back of the book

44

A good deal of this is because the systems which we use to support us are deeply entrenched in medical model thinking. They rely on assessments by professionals. There are two main types of assessments. Those designed to find out just how impaired your child is, and the second is to find out if they fit the criteria for services. These criteria are usually based on what is wrong with your child and what they cannot do, and to make it even worse, they change constantly as the local authority or the Government changes its' funding priorities or the law changes. They are usually forms to be filled in over and over again, each time reinforcing everything negative you ever thought or felt about your child. Often they are filled in by professionals who have no relationship with your child and do not take into account the fact that all our needs are relative to the situation we are in. For example, when I am at home in my own house where everything is adapted for me, I need very little additional physical help. However, if I go away to a different environment I might need 24 hr support because it is not adapted or accessible to me.

Disabled adults have learned to treat the whole thing for what it is. Find out what the criteria are for the things you need and answer the questions accordingly. Rosaleen advises:

"Become assertive. If you are not already an assertive person, then I would seriously recommend that you sign up for the first 'Assertiveness course' that you come across. You will need to be assertive to be able to deal with all of the bureaucracy, red tape, prejudice, barriers, discrimination and downright ignorance that you will have to tolerate. If you can deal with people in an assertive but non-aggressive way you are more likely to be successful in your outcomes and in meeting your goals."
Rosaleen Moriarty- Simmonds

Speaking from experience, it will be worth it in the end. It is amazing how much stress falls away when the right supports are in place. That may be the beginning of your ability to start enjoying your child, and needless to say they will be very pleased for that. One area of change which must be fought for is to redesign assessments according to the social model. This is very slowly beginning to happen under the direction of 'Person-Centred Planning' and self-assessment.

One word of warning – be careful to not become too dependent on the resources your child may bring into the household because of his/her impairment. As they grow older, the ownership of these resources, except perhaps Carer's Allowance, will transfer to them. You do not want to get into a situation where young adults feel trapped at home in order to prop up the family income, or worse still, they are never allowed to take control of their own money.

Brothers and Sisters

"The worst effect of my experiences as a child was the feeling that I didn't belong. I was a different creature - the separation from my siblings from which we have never recovered."
John Ley

For many of you your disabled child will not be your only child. The medical model will have its part to play in how your children relate to each other, how you relate to them, and the importance the world places on nurturing the relationships between the young people.

The worst thing that could happen is a complete separation of the disabled child from his/her family. Some parents decide they cannot look after a disabled child and either put them into full-time institutional care, or put them up for adoption. Without knowing the individual circumstances it is impossible to judge whether this was a good decision or not as this happens to non-disabled children at times for their own safety. However, it is a pretty safe bet to say that no one would willingly give up their child if they were given the support they need to be a parent. It is also a certainty that that separation will affect everyone concerned for the rest of their lives, however good the alternative arrangements are. The separation of brothers and sisters is often an overlooked dimension of this. Having listened to a talk about the Eugenics Movement and the history of segregation for disabled people, Maresa speaks of her realisation that, when she was fostered and then adopted, not only did she lose her brother, four years older than herself, but he lost her:

"I was a wanted baby, the second child with an older brother. At first all they could see was that I had a club foot, but even this, maybe, distanced my mother from me. When I was a few months old, my parents noticed I was not developing in a typical way, and couldn't sit by myself, amongst other things. So when I was ten months old, I was assessed and found to have Cerebral Palsy. Only a week after this diagnosis, my parents decided they couldn't look after me, so I went to live with a foster family.

Although my memories are very hazy, I think I knew I couldn't be what they wanted, but my brother loved me as I was. We were forced to be separate against our wills, both of us. That is what hurts me more than anything, what it did to my closeness with my brother. That is what makes me so angry, that (eugenics) history is my history. I was taken away from my brother who loved me. I think my parents had already withdrawn, so the diagnosis was just the last straw.

Since then, although I have been loved, the yearning for the love that was taken away has never left me, and I still yearn. For twenty years I was a secret, and clearly never spoken of to my brother. He was forced to forget me, and it was only after six years of my asking, that my mother eventually told my brother, and my younger sister, of my existence. Last year I met my mother, brother and sister, but they were so distant.

Hearing that history makes me less angry with my parents but more angry with a system that can undermine the essence of humanity. After the original separation from my birth family, for a further ten years in the education system, I was again forced apart from other young people which, in its turn, has made us frightened of each other, except for a few exceptions.

To me the history is still there in a huge way. The walls of conditional acceptance are still there. We must break them. If my brother and I are ever going to reclaim our relationship, those walls of conditions must be knocked down. What has all this done to him? My first disappearing, then silence. What has he buried and become fearful of?"
Maresa Mackeith

When I was a child growing up in the 1950s, I spent a lot of time in hospital. It was policy then to not allow children under 12 as visitors into the children's wards because they brought in "too many germs". This meant that I did not see my older sister for weeks at a time, and it had a very damaging effect on our relationship. Chris speaks of similar difficulties:

"(My hospitalisations) also had a bad effect on relationship with my siblings. (I had had an extremely close relationship with my sisters up to that point.) I believe they became jealous of the amount of 'attention' I was receiving and started to bully me. In those days, siblings were not allowed on hospital wards and I missed them terribly when I was hospitalised several times for what turned out to be completely unnecessary operations. Whenever I got out of hospital we would be further separated by the fact that they had grown closer to each other whilst I had been away.

I would have liked my parents to think about the situation between me and my sisters and, instead of telling them off for bullying me, figure out a way to help me get them back."
Chris O' Mahony

It is very difficult to prevent your disabled child from appearing to be more important than your other children, especially to them. They seem to need so much more attention, they cause a lot of worry and may seem 'favoured'. The non-disabled child(ren) may feel tremendous pressure to be the 'successful' one, or may feel they would only be loved if they too were disabled. Some are made to feel that they will be expected to take over the parent's role when they die which, at the time, can loom ahead like a life sentence. All this of course can cause a great deal of fear, resentment and jealousy.

Children have a strong sense of natural justice and will resent what feels like different treatment amongst their siblings. One of the things I remember thinking was good when I was a child was that my parents generally applied the same rules to me as to my sister with only slight adaptations to accommodate my 'special needs'. For example, when my parents thought we were being cheeky or disobedient my sister got smacked, but because they did not want to break my bones, I got my hair pulled instead! We both got sent to our rooms for being naughty, but I got carried up to mine whereas she had to climb the stairs herself. When my mother decided she had done enough ironing and we were going to have to do our own, I was not exempted although it took me a lot longer and we had to buy a lightweight iron. This of course helped unite us children in the face of the horrible adults, and I liked it. Children in general need to feel close to other young people, especially those in their own family.

In some families the brothers and sisters are the disabled child's best friends and allies. Nancy remembers her early life as one disabled girl amongst four non-disabled brothers:

"I was the only girl and very happy in the company of my brothers. Every year we went on a seaside caravan holiday, playing with our Lowestoft cousins Frances and Paul, and at Whitsun on marathon cycling holidays. For a while Mick and I rode tandem together, his strong legs like tree trunks, powering us both as we ate up the miles... as I grew up I became gradually disabled, finally having to use a wheelchair, but this was never allowed to be an obstacle in the pursuit of our adventures. If there was a flight of stairs in our way, Mick would straight away be carting me up it – we climbed up castles, towers and battlements and down narrow stone steps into cellars and crypts.

An abiding memory is of the fantastic holiday I had with Phil and Mick in Venice. Mick delighting in rushing around, up and down the stepped bridges, racing me with my wheelchair against the locals with their carts and trolleys.

Another gem was the weekend the three of us travelled to North Wales. Despite horrible cold and windy weather, we embarked upon a heroic assent of Mount Snowdon, Mick and Phil carrying me between them in my wheelchair. When I was with them it seemed like there was nothing I couldn't do. Just the other day I found a photograph that Mick took of me sitting in my wheelchair, gazing out from the summit of an alpine peak, eating the sausages he had ingeniously contrived to cook inside the engine of our struggling overheated car."
Nancy Willis

They may well be the ones who create a path for the child out into the wider world with more skill and ability than any adult could muster because they have the local contacts and speak the language of young people.

When trying to balance the needs of all your children, a good starting point is a reality check. I have been alive for over half a century so I have a longer view. Although there still are children abandoned in institutions, or left alone and neglected at home, the situation for most disabled children in the developed world is like a dream compared to our past. If your child knows they are loved, they already have more than many. If they have a roof over their head, warm clothes and enough food to eat, they are doing well. If they have cuddles and health care when they are ill, toys to play with and are stimulated to learn they are amongst the worlds most privileged. If they have technological equipment such as computers, wheelchairs or speech machines when they need them, it is good to remember that most disabled people in the world who need such things don't have them. The problems which disabled children face such as rejection and loneliness are also felt by many others, especially in our modern materialistic world. I am not trying to dismiss the struggles you are probably having to support your child to do well, I am asking you to make sure you have things in proportion, especially in regard to the struggles of your other children.

A helpful thing, many families have found is to introduce the idea of 'Special Time' into their daily lives. This means deciding to spend a specific amount of time with each of their children, one-by-one, not together, during which time the child decides what they are all going to do (within the bounds of safety and expense). It must be the same amount of time for each child, including the disabled child, and it must be stuck to. It may only be half an hour a week, one Saturday a month, or whatever is realistic for your family, but obviously, the longer it is the better. For a child to have this reliable bit of undivided attention which is about their needs can bring a remarkable sense of safety. To begin with they may test the parent - ask them to play all the games they hate, or go to the shops and buy loads of sweets. If the parent goes along with it however, they will gradually use it to share with them all sorts of concerns and worries. They will feel they matter as much as anyone else and will not feel they are fighting all the time to get heard. Nor will they continue to feel hopeless and withdrawn if that is how they generally respond the probing questions of adults.

The Minefield of Therapy

It is very hard to think clearly about therapy and treatments, especially when you are making decisions for someone else. There is a 'medical model' of therapy, and a 'social model' of therapy. The medical model approach puts a great emphasis on 'normalization', i.e. getting disabled children to talk, walk, sit, move look like, behave like and sound like non-disabled children, as if this has made them 'better'. These interventions have included breaking and stretching the bones of people with achondroplasia (dwarfism) to make them a few inches taller, amputating parts of children's limbs to make them fit better into artificial legs or arms, forcing children to walk with braces, jackets and crutches when they would have been much more able to get around in a wheelchair, tying deaf children's hands to their chairs in order to stop them using their native sign languages and trying to learn to speak instead, performing plastic surgery on the eyes of children with Downs syndrome and the highly controversial use of powerful drugs such as Ritalin to modify children's behaviour so that they can fit into rigid systems. Many of us have suffered enormously from the imposition of such 'treatments'. As adults we have found that many of our impairments have become worse because of them, especially damage to joints and ligaments from being forced to move in ways which were unnatural to us, or from the long-term effects of drugs which were not researched well enough.

The social model approach is different in that its goal is not 'normalization' but empowerment. A 'social model' speech therapist will not be so concerned with a child's speech or diction, but with their overall ability to communicate with others, and others with them. Such a speech therapist might introduce a non-verbal child to 'Facilitated Communication' or help them obtain, programme and use assistive technology which can speak for them.

A social model physiotherapist is less interested in cajoling your child to labour all day pushing a manual wheelchair as a form of exercise, than assisting your child to do the things they want with the help of technology, friends and personal assistants, including keeping healthy. A social model Occupational Therapist will be less interested in rehabilitation through arts and crafts, than finding ways to support your child's chosen lifestyle and interests with useful aids and adaptations to their environments. Medical model therapists usually see themselves as experts, hold on to their knowledge and follow their own goals. Social model therapist usually see themselves a facilitators, like to pass on as much information to their clients as possible, and will try to find out a child's goals. Edwina recounts her experience of both therapeutic models starting with the medical:

"I went to a day special school in Kingston. I hated it. They put me in callipers...I didn't want to wear my callipers. I could crawl and get around better without them. They were horrible. My mum stopped putting them on and she got into trouble for it.

*School wasn't about social skills and speech. It was about walking all the f*****g time. I was persuaded to have operations to straighten my legs so I could walk. I wanted to do it to please my mum and dad. I thought that if I could walk I wouldn't be a disappointment any more. But the operations stopped me being able to crawl and I was actually less mobile. Walking makes me totally knackered. It's a no-no for me."*

In contrast she describes an intervention that was very useful to her:

"I loved speech therapy. It taught me to breathe properly and to cough, to eat and swallow, and they don't hurt you. They let you blow bubbles to get control. They don't say they are going to make you perfect. They taught me techniques to speak, but speech is more about confidence and emotions. It's also to do with other people's attitudes."
Edwina Macarthy

Sapna expressed a great deal of anger about the lack of physiotherapy which she needed as a young child and as she grew older, despite being in a 'special' school. Like many of us she has had to get her needs met privately. This she believes is wrong:

"Physiotherapy, like education should be a fundamental human right for every child with special needs but in reality children are less likely to get physiotherapy as they grow older with disastrous consequences.

I currently have regular physiotherapy and Yoga which are supported by my Dad of course. Parents, like mine, just need the right advice and guidance for their child, but this is rare. It is therefore up to parents to find their own answers to problems that they face with their special needs child and to realise that limitations are often caused by lack of self-confidence and 'professionals' providing advice based on their

perceptions which are often wrong. Remember, you, as a parent, know your child best, do not be afraid to demand human rights for your child with special needs.

Sapna Ramnani

The interesting thing is that most funding goes to the medical model approach rather than the social model approach. Inclusive practice is based on the social model, but there is still a big struggle to drag the resources from the old, institutionalised provision to the new. It is not just a question of redeploying staff from segregated 'special' provision into mainstream settings. They need retraining in the social model approach or they themselves become a barrier to inclusion.

Faced with all sorts of pressures, contradictory advice and stressful situations, it is not easy to sort out what is to be avoided, and what is to be fought for. You will probably make mistakes. We all did. With the benefit of hindsight I would say that, unless your child is in a life or death situation try not to make decisions on their behalf which they will not be able to reverse when they are older.

In the end, our bodies are our own. Even though they may be unusual shapes or sizes, and sometimes hurt us, generally we are pretty fond of them. It is up to us to weigh up the pros and cons of changing them and your task as a parent is to help us be in control of this most basic element of ourselves. Doctors are not gods and you can say NO.

The Developmental Curriculum

Many professionals who will be involved with you in the early years will be deeply steeped in the training they received on child development and how this relates to children who are not 'normal', however there are big discussions to be had on this subject.

We are still learning every day about our bodies and how they work. We know even less about our minds and how things outside of themselves affect them. Not knowing things however is not our biggest problem. The real problem is thinking we know things when we don't. Ill or disabled people have been at the receiving end of diagnoses, treatments, programmes, therapies, services and imposed life styles dreamed up by non-disabled professionals who have often been driven more by guesswork than fact.

At the time of course, given the information available to people, many of the treatments seemed to make sense, at least to the people proposing them. For example in the 4th century BC, Hippocrates pronounced on the achieving of the proper balance between the four humours of the body that:

"The body of man has in itself blood, phlegm, yellow bile and black bile. These make up the nature of his body and through these he feels pain or enjoys health. Now he enjoys the most perfect health when these elements are duly proportioned to one another in respect of compounding power or bulk, and when they are perfectly mingled. Pain is felt when one of these elements is in deficit or excess, or is isolated in the body without being compounded in the body with all the others"

It was believed that these humours were directly associated with distinct emotional states:

Blood of the heart – cheerfulness; optimism

Phlegm of the brain – calm, unemotional

Yellow bile of the liver – irritable, easily angered

Black bile of the spleen – melancholy, gloomy, pensive

These assumptions led to many treatments which seem barbaric to us in hindsight – leeches for example stuck all over our bodies to suck out our excess blood. Even when new information makes these ideas outdated, they tend to live on through the generations, becoming diluted but not disappearing entirely, clouding our thinking for a long time. Think how our language still reflects the notion of humours, such as the word 'phlegmatic', or the phrases 'heartfelt', or 'he was in a black mood'. Now we know a bit more but that 'knowing' did not come overnight, nor was it accepted without resistance from the followers of the original theories. The same is true today. One relic of the medical model we are finding hard to shake off is the 'Developmental Curriculum'.

The developmental curriculum seems logical. Based on much observation and research into the usual pattern of the development of children, it was noticed that most children followed the same path, or sequence of gaining skills, i.e. turns towards, sound – reaches out with whole hand – smiles in response to familiar faces – develops pincer movement with thumb and finger etc, etc. It was thought that all children had to develop along this straight line of development – that they could not miss a step or progress in any area without completing all the levels, like a programmed computer game. This assumption has led to one of the biggest man-made barriers to learning that disabled children have had to face. Much of 'Special Education' is based on this idea. Trying to be helpful, adults have held disabled children locked to the things they cannot do, or cannot do well, believing that only when they learn to do it can they move on to the next stage, or skill.

The result is the same as it would be for anyone who was forced to concentrate all their effort on the things that for them are really difficult, or impossible – frustration, boredom, disengaging and sometimes exploding. In the long term it leads to a massive underachievement, loss of confidence and sense of personal inadequacy and failure. Simone is a passionate advocate for people like herself who have been labelled from early childhood as having learning difficulties. She describes her frustration with the developmental curriculum and its associated assessments and tests:

"When I was born there was an expectation that I could access and

participate in the many opportunities which are available to everyone. This is because I believe mum and dad would have just accepted me for who I was. But all this was dashed away when the professionals got out their rulers to measure how well I was doing in comparison with so called 'normal' people. My life was turned upside down, being sent to a residential special school from the age of 4 until 16 simply because my mum and dad did not snatch this ruler from the doctors who were convinced that their standardized tests were right, meaning some children could have their normal human needs met whilst others won't.

In the residential special school, (prison), I received little education. I had few Maths lessons even though I was good at Maths, whilst having plenty of English lessons and Physiotherapy. No real humanities or science - a curriculum which really leaves you with few choices - domestic science, Jewish Studies and lots of meaningless independence living stuff without context. And during the weekends nought was on offer other than boring walks in the woods, silent reading and praying to a God. Occasionally, we were allowed to visit Chester when everything was closed on Sunday!

The whole education training was more about preparation for a life of exploitation and passively accepting that things will be done to you rather than one of being a critical active citizen, ready to make a mark on the world. And did not special schooling half 'screw up' my relationship with my family as how can one be developed if most of the year you were not living at home?"
Simone Apsis

Jackie's story shows many parallels:

"My mother brought up the five of us on her own. She knew I was a slower learner than my brothers and sisters and she tried to protect me by just encouraging me to do what I could.

It still upsets me to remember the day when I was called out of the class at my mainstream school. I was about seven. There was a man in a suit who didn't know me. I had never seen him before. He gave me tests I had never *seen and that day his judgements shattered my life. He met me for one day and didn't even say goodbye. He said I had to go to a special school after that. Where is your human rights in that? I felt stupid, backwards, like an idiot with no sense. I was ashamed. Everyone else I knew went to a proper school.*

The psychologist was like a doctor saying you have to be sectioned. No one argues with doctors do they, because they don't understand what they are saying. My mother was from an afro-Caribbean background where she was the oldest child. This meant that she had to stay home and help to look after the other children, so she did not go to school and could not read and write. I think this made her scared of authority figures and whatever they suggested, she said 'Yes' to everything.

What I wish is that my Mum and I had had independent advocates when I was a child who could have helped us understand what the suits were telling us. I wish the school I was in had just taken more time to help me develop my learning and used more creative ways, not just pen and paper"
Jackie Downer MBE

If parents are not too heavily swayed by the tests, their own observations often seem to point in a very different direction. While it may be true that most children do develop along similar lines (although there is a wide variation between children considered to be normal), where there are stumbling blocks caused by some physical impairment, intellectual or neurological difference then children can find another way, or develop other skills, much more like a fan than a straight line.

There is a growing body of anecdotal and statistical evidence of this, the most dramatic coming from disabled young people who have been enabled to communicate through assistive technology or Facilitated Communication. Many of these young people were assessed as having stopped developing at an infantile level because they were unable to perform expected tasks or tests due to their physical limitations. This usually included the co-ordination necessary to speak. However, with the right support, these

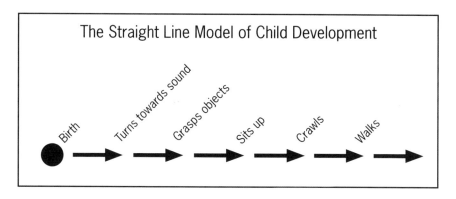

The Straight Line Model of Child Development

Birth → Turns towards sound → Grasps objects → Sits up → Crawls → Walks

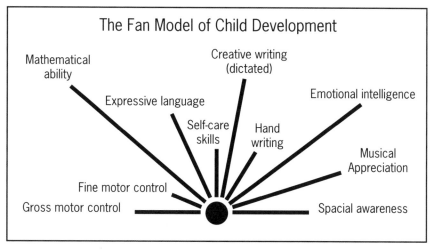

The Fan Model of Child Development

Mathematical ability
Creative writing (dictated)
Expressive language
Emotional intelligence
Self-care skills
Hand writing
Musical Appreciation
Fine motor control
Gross motor control
Spacial awareness

same young people demonstrated the ability to decode symbols including the alphabet and to point to them. They were thus able to read, write and express opinions, sometimes of a most profound and thoughtful nature.

Maresa Mackeith is non-verbal and only learned to communicate via Facilitated Communication when she was nine. Until then it had been deemed that her intellectual and physical development was stuck at the level of an eighteen month old child primarily because of her physical inability to perform the tests to prove otherwise. Despite her use of FC at home with many different facilitators, her special school never accepted that her communications were valid. Maresa says:

"I am a Special School Survivor, mistakes were made with me. It was ordinary teachers and ordinary young people, who had the confidence to listen to me. Yes, we need expertise. I needed an unusual speech therapist, who had had to leave her job in the system, so she could gain the skills she needed to help me. We need the expertise in the context of real inclusion, not added on to an already selective system of who is worth teaching and who is not. I was not considered worth teaching."
Maresa Mackeith

The linear model leads to assuming that a child needs a pared down curriculum focussing on small steps of progress especially in their areas of difficulty; the fan model leads to assuming that a child needs a highly stimulating environment in which they are enabled to make choices, discover and develop all their unblocked areas of ability and interest, thought and feeling even if they have great difficulty with self-expression. The linear model is the medical model. The fan model is the social model. Simone continues with her advice to parents:

"It would be fantastic if you could snatch that ruler out of the professional's hands before it goes anyway near your child. This ruler blocked my mum and dad seeing me as a full human being with 'normal needs' of love, acceptance and a sense of belonging in our local community. And you just accept everyone best learns in different ways and will acquire new knowledge, skills and reach milestones at different times of lives - and dare I even say it – may never complete a milestone at all – but it really does not matter.

Look for all the gifts that your child has and help to nurture them. Whilst your child may struggle in one area, make sure everything else is still available to him or her. Focusing simply on reducing or eliminating a weakness will do nothing to enhance your child's esteem and value themselves for who they are.

Before I go, the most liberating thing you can do is to snatch that professional's ruler and give your child a full life, surrounding by your loving family, neighbours and friends within their local community."
Simone Aspis

Sapna also speaks about the need to not be intimidated by the negativity of assessments:

"It must be frightening for parents to be told by 'professionals' that your child would not walk or talk but it is up to the individual parents to help their child disabled or not to realise their potential and not for others to set a benchmark for the child. Your child will be defined by their own limitations and not those of other people or even yourselves and this applies to non-disabled kids as well."
Sapna Ramnani

On the other hand, Cornelia, a parent, talks about how her own lack of knowledge of child development led her to expect things of her son which were not possible at the stages he had so far reached. She reminds us again that listening to the child is key:

"I am thinking about the real challenge of supporting the development of Luc for example (a child with Down's Syndrome). His system did not seem to initiate the process of learning. It seemed that we had to teach him that learning is a thing that humans do right from when he was tiny. I needed to affirm quite consciously that crying is a good thing to do when you are hungry and want mum's attention and her nipple!

We seemed in an extremely powerful position as we truly had to guide Luc through processes which ordinary children often do spontaneously.

Some ideas about developmental stages were really helpful, because I did find myself several times in places where I was expecting something of Luc that he couldn't do yet and was in danger of undermining his confidence. I was glad of some therapist, portage worker or teacher telling me to stop and suggest something else to Luc.

So I learned the vital ingredient is listening to the child, which of course with a small baby is observing: noticing any responses, any minute changes in expression or movement or body tension.

Theories of development can form a supportive structure, if the adult understands himself as an initiator only, a facilitator; always listening and observing and creating possibilities for the child to be able to take the next step; always working with the understanding that the child is in charge of the learning process and the eventual outcomes".
Cornelia Broesskamp

Boredom

As a child we want and need our parents to protect us. As a parent we feel instinctively drawn to protect our children. We share this with most animal life. It is a very deep and pro-life part of our nature. When one of our children is ill, or otherwise seemingly in danger, our protective instincts go into overdrive. When our child is permanently disabled this protective instinct can become locked in the 'on' position, even when things are relatively safe. Many of the services that have been developed for disabled children also have this notion of safety very high on the agenda. Although it is not the intention, for a child this can result in a life which is very restricted and boring. Coupled with the pared down learning environment designed by supporters of 'Special Education' with the doctrine of the Developmental Curriculum, the overlooking of our inner life, the barriers in society to accessing mainstream children's social activities, not to mention the hours children have to spend hanging around waiting for adults to help them do things, this boredom can become crushing. Ali describes the effect of an unstimulating curriculum in his special school:

"Boredom was a big part of my childhood. I could grasp the end result of a two-hour lesson in the first five minutes."
Ali Kashmiri

It could be argued that all young people in the 'rich' world are suffering from overprotection and consequent boredom. It maybe explains why so many teenagers start taking wild risks with sex, drugs and fighting with dangerous weapons, or decide to go on what, to their parents, look like suicide missions in their gap years. Indeed many adults risk their lives engaging in activities such as climbing mountains or speeding in cars rather than experience the flatness of a safe life without these challenges. No one steps in to stop them if they are not endangering other people. We accept that adults are responsible for shaping their own lives – unless they need help from other people to do it.

Boredom was by far the most harmful aspect of my experience of growing up in the 1950s as a disabled child. I spent many weeks lying in hospital cots or beds, not allowed to get up and play with the other children even when my fractures were healed, for fear that I would get another injury. I was not allowed to go to school for the same reason. I still find it hard to express the pain of having nothing to do and no one to play with. I remember being pushed around the shops with my mother and passing the noisy playground of my sister's school from which I had been excluded. I remember thinking that I would rather have sat all day in the back of a classroom, ignored and unable to go to the toilet in order to be able to watch and listen to the young life around me. I would rather have broken more bones having fun than fewer bones sitting alone at home. I suspected already that their fears were much more for themselves being held responsible for an accident, than for me. I had a home tutor for eight hours a week, the rest of the time was empty space. I do not remember anyone thinking that this was an issue or asking me what I felt about it.

But even then I could see that some children had it worse. I could at least occupy myself. I could read, play with my toys, knit and sew, make things with construction kits or modelling materials. I could hear the radio – children's hour was a favourite – and I could paint and draw, activities in which I gradually became 'lost' for many hours a day. I can hardly imagine what it is like for children who are not given access to the material resources I used – books, toys, paper and pencils – or who cannot initiate or carryout such activities because of a greater level of impairment. I can well imagine the desperate behaviour and even mental breakdown that could result if no one comes to help. Or the slow withering of mental ability as a leg withers if it is never stood upon. I have seen haunting television images of disabled children in institutions in Eastern Europe who are still living and dying in this particular hell, but there are children and young people in my country who are also experiencing such deprivation. It is possible for disabled young people and young adults to become institutionalised within their own homes.

Life is about risk and I was very clear as a child, that it is better to die 'living' than live a half-life. And to state the obvious, the greater your level of impairment, the greater your dependence on others to create varied and stimulating environments in which you can grow and develop - the very opposite of institutional life.

The Art of Listening

The first thing, as with all parents, is to learn to listen to your child. I have not met a disabled child yet who has not had opinions – things they like and things they don't like. I have not met a child who has not tried to express those opinions, or choices somehow – through body language, expressions of emotion, or language. Some parents notice and respond to these attempts at communication. Others find it harder.

Perhaps much depends on how well 'listened to' they have been themselves. This does not mean adults have to do everything a child wants, but it means acknowledging that they do (or don't) want something, and letting them know you have understood what it is. Sometimes you will not be able to co-operate with the child's wishes, but you can still 'listen' to their upset about it, including their tears and anger.

There seems to be a particular difficulty for parents of disabled children around listening to their child's upsets or tears. Some of this has come from the institutionalising of disabled children when the desire of the professionals was to make everyone believe it was a good thing and that the children were happy even when they weren't. Mary Harrison speaks of her first memories:

"My first memory of boarding school is standing in the school hallway with Matron holding my hand and bending down to whisper in my ear 'Don't let Mummy see you cry'. Mum and Dad were walking away looking strained and uncomfortable. The realisation that I was not going back home with them had caused an almighty lump to form in my throat which was truly painful and was demanding to be relieved by crying. I did what I was told, however, by Matron and saved my tears until I was under the covers in bed in a dormitory full of other sobbing young children. I was five years old.

At the beginning of each term the same thing happened, except that I no longer had to be told 'don't let mummy see you cry'. At each parting from my parents the misery of being wrenched from my parents and home became an inexorable and dreaded feature of my young life. My childhood grief was private and only expressed under the bedclothes on the first night of each term. During the following days I entered into the life of the school doing the best I could in a resigned and miserable sort of way. Because I didn't cry in front of people everyone assumed I was happy. My mother recently told me that when all the parents and children gathered at Waterloo Station waiting to get on the train that took us to school, I would go round comforting all the children. Needless to say I have no recollection of this, but it must illustrate how good I was at putting on a brave face. My mother doesn't know to this day how miserable I was.

I wish my parents had known then that it was alright for me to cry but in the 1950s, the British stiff upper lip was still all-pervasive. The bulldog spirit still reigned supreme and at five year old I was its number one example. Nowadays of course we all know that crying is a healthy and normal route to healing emotional pain and that if a child cries uncontrollably it is quite normal. Asking a child not to cry is like asking a bird not to sing. I think the consequence of this early experience is that I have always found it difficult to express grief - especially in front of my mother - even though I feel it as keenly as the next person, but there is always a little voice in me that says 'don't let mummy see you cry' (whether she's with me or not). That is not to say I never cry, of course, but it is almost always done in private with no witnesses and under extreme provocation.

My brother, Phil, went to the same school too and I suspect it was even worse for him, being male and more severely disabled. Again my mother used to say 'big boys don't cry' and 'what a baby' if he burst into tears."
Mary Harrison

Paying a child warm attention whilst they cry, or express anger or fear is a very powerful healing tool. We could all do with more of it. Crying, laughing, raging, sweating and yawning are all signs of our bodies and minds healing from hurts, physical and emotional. This is also true of talking, something that is more 'allowed' in our present cultures, which explains why some people can't seem to stop as soon as they find a listening ear!

Apart from listening to your child, the next step on their road to empowerment is to learn how to make choices. The important thing is that however tiny or trivial the choices are, they must be real, in that you can act on your child's decisions. For example, when my daughter was very young, I asked her if she wanted her toast cut in squares or triangles, and she always had a preference. Or I would offer her the choice of clothes to wear, or whether she wanted her hair in a ponytail or bunches. If your child can indicate his/her choices by pointing, looking, smiling, signing or speaking makes no difference. The more choices you can offer in a day the better. What your child will learn is that she can expect support for his/her own decisions. This is the building block for independence later on.

As you child grows older, and you expand the scope of his/her choices, you will be faced by her making what, in your mind, will be the 'wrong' choice. It may lead to failure, or disappointment or some other consequence your child will have to sort out. Allowing your child to make mistakes and learn from them is also a building block of independence. We all need to be allowed to get things wrong without fear of other people's judgement or humiliation. Your useful role will be to help them to use the experience to make different choices in the future. Rosaleen reminds us of the importance of encouragement:

"Always give your disabled child lots of encouragement. They need to know that you are supporting them in whatever it is they choose to do. These could be minor and simple everyday tasks or huge momentous experiences. But the difference between you encouraging them and not encouraging could be 'failure'. None of us want to set our children up to fail, we want to support them, nurture them, guide and advise them so that they become empowered young people.
Rosaleen Moriarty-Simmonds

It can take any of us a long time to know what we want to do with our lives. Usually we have to try lots of things first. Disabled young people may find it harder to do this discovering for many reasons. They may find new situations scary and stressful and so opt for familiarity and safety. Or there might be lots of barriers in the way of doing what they want.

Disabled young people who need physical support or facilitation have a particularly hard time doing things that are not approved of by their 'carers' unlike their non-disabled peers. This is why young friends are so important. Independence cannot truly happen if you are too scared of other people's disapproval.

The Listening Partnership

Being able to give your child attention to develop their own thinking will depend on how much attention you yourself have been given in the past, and how much you get now in order to help you deal with your own needs.

Although we are not generally in the habit, it is really easy to turn any good relationship into a dynamic 'listening' partnership. The secret is to take turns. However little time you have, divide it into half. For one half ask your partner to listen to you while you talk, think, cry, laugh, thump a pillow, or whatever you need to do. Ask them not to be judgemental, give you advice, change the subject or interrupt you with their own stories. Tell them you are downloading a lot of stuff that is getting in the way of your thinking straight. When the first half time is over change places. Treat these exchanges as confidential and do not refer to the 'other' persons issues later unless they bring them up themselves, however much you want to. You will be amazed at the difference such 'attention' can make. And you will understand better why your children need it.

(If you want to expand your understanding and practice of this exchange of 'time' read 'Listening to Children' and 'The Listening Partnership' detailed at the end of this book. There is an international organisation which runs classes and workshops based on this theory in many countries including the UK. People who have taken classes and want to continue to develop their skills can join a local community of others, if there is one near you. To find out more look up www.rc.org. It stands for Re-Evaluation Co-Counselling. There is much work done in this community around supporting children and young people as well as their parents.)

There is another sort of listening which may be even more challenging - taking notice of what your children say and acting on it. This is not what we are expected to do with our non-disabled children, never mind our disabled ones. And who took any notice of us when we were children?

Some parents deal with the difficulties in their family life by being overly controlling. It seems like the only way to survive, and of course many disabled children (but not all!) are easier to control than their brothers and sisters because they are less mobile, slower, or more dependent on your help to do things, or even to speak. In the long term however, it will benefit both you and your child if you can gradually empower them to take control of their own lives as much as possible. Many disabled adults now live independent lives using the support of paid Personal Assistants. Learning how to manage this kind of support is a life-skill which needs to be gradually learned from childhood. This will require you sometimes letting them direct you instead of the other way round.

Maresa reminds us that there is even another level of listening, perhaps the hardest of all. Those of us who experience life from the margins can sometimes see things others can't:

"Listen to us, we can teach you.
I think if you don't, the world is truly on its way to destruction."
Maresa Mackeith

Empowerment

The revolution which has begun to happen for disabled people around the world is that we are regaining the control over our own lives. For much of the past the fact that we often needed resources or physical help from other people, coupled with our low status in society, has meant that our lives have been controlled by the people who provide that help – parents, carers, services, charities, managers of schools, homes and day centres, doctors and therapists, local and central government. It seemed that the only way to have any choice or control was to not need that help – to become 'independent'. Obviously that couldn't work for everyone, and even for those of us who could just about manage with a lot of struggle and effort, it still limited our lives and tired us out. The medical model of disability has encouraged this notion of 'independence' because it is cheap. If we don't need help then no one has to pay for it. Much of 'special education' has traditionally been about a high level of input whilst someone is young from therapists and teachers of 'life skills', with the hope that they will become adults who can get by without paid help. Parents are easily persuaded to collaborate with this programme because it sounds good. It seems to make sense. After all, most non-disabled people learn to limit their lives to the things they can do without help and feel that that is how things should be. Only the rich are expected to have nannies and housekeepers, gardeners and chauffeurs because they can pay for it themselves.

Parents of non disabled children tend to take it for granted that their job is to help them take control of their lives step by step until the time they are no longer dependent on them. They assume however that they will be caring for their disabled children even when they are adults.

Disabled people however have thought a great deal about this and have a different view:

> All human beings depend on each other in reality. No one is truly 'independent'.

> We need help, AND we need to direct it. This leads to true 'independence'.

When we get that sort of assistance we are able to develop our personalities, interests and gifts, becoming contributors to society rather than 'burdens'.

When the barriers to inclusion are removed from people's thinking, environments and services, the extra help we need is much less than when the barriers are in place.

If we cannot manage the 'paperwork' then we should be able to choose who we trust to manage it for us.

"An Empowered disabled person is: open to change; assertive; proactive; self-accountable; uses their feelings; is self-directed; learns by their own mistakes; confronts situations; lives in the present; is realistic; thinks in relative terms and has high self esteem. Of course a disabled person who is not empowered has all of the opposite characteristics. As a parent or guardian it is your duty to empower your child."
Rosaleen Moriarty-Simmonds

Empowering technology

I have met many parents who seemed to find it difficult to welcome technology into the lives of their disabled children, especially the bigger things like powered wheelchairs or electronic speech aids. Perhaps they seem like symbols of failure, being forced to accept that your child is one of 'those' children. To disabled people however technology is truly liberating. We love it. For many of us our lives have been truly transformed by the right bit of kit. Apart from mobility and speech aids, there are ever-improving computer programmes for children with visual impairments and even for non-readers (the computer speaks and the child dictates their response into a microphone). Finding out about it and getting it are still problems because much of it is expensive. Don't sit and wait for the OT to knock on your door with a bunch of catalogues and an order form. Do your own research and go for the best. There are many children's charities which can help financially.

Giving Your Child Information About Themselves

All people with impairments, including children, need to know everything about their impairment, so that they have real insight and knowledge about themselves and their needs. It is a crucial part of their empowerment. Not having this information is never useful, especially if the impairment is 'hidden'. Luke Jackson, a thirteen year old boy with Asperger Syndrome devotes several pages to this issue in his book 'Freaks, Geeks and Asperger Syndrome':

"I first found out I had Asperger Syndrome from an article in The Guardian that Julia gave Mum to show me. It was about Asperger Syndrome and about how Albert Einstein was supposed to have had it. It told how many people with Asperger Syndrome have been very successful in their lives. One of the people is Bill Gates, the director of Microsoft. Although these weren't actually diagnosed, they were recognised to have 'traits' of AS. The article had checklists of certain behaviours that were considered to be traits of Asperger Syndrome.

I was twelve years old when I read this article. Mum had plonked it in front of me as if she had done it by accident. She knows that I read everything and anything. As I read through the article my first reaction was relief. It was as if I had a weight lifted off my shoulders. I had every single 'symptom on this checklist. I read it and reread it, then said to my Mum 'Do you think I could have AS?' She simply said 'Yes you have'. I must admit that I did think 'Thanks a lot for telling me,' but the relief was most definitely stronger than the annoyance (at that time anyway).

I had finally found the reason why other people classed me as clumsy or stupid. My heart lightened instantly and the constant nagging that had accompanied me all my life (not my Mum) stopped immediately. I finally knew why I felt different, why I felt as if I was a freak, why I didn't seem to fit in. Even better, it was not my fault!

"If the child get taken to see doctors and other people and the parents talk in whispered conversations about them and tell the child nothing, then that is denying the child the right to know about themselves".

"I can't stress enough how bugged I was to 'discover' my AS at least five years after I was actually diagnosed. Mum could have saved me a lot of years of worry because I always knew I was different. When I asked Mum why she had not told me for such a long time about AS she said that she was bothered that I may read up on it and start to experience 'symptoms' I didn't actually have. I think this was very stupid! I do wonder whether she thought I would grow out of it too."
Luke Jackson

Another advantage of giving your child good information is that it is much easier for a disabled child to make friends and allies of other children if they are 'empowered' to explain their impairments and their needs, without shame:

"A child came from another school to Turves Green Primary School because she had been teased about having Cystic Fibrosis. She asked me, the Head Teacher, to tell everybody about her – to tell them about her impairment. We agreed to stand together in assembly and she told everyone, and she never had an issue with people teasing her in our school."
Head Teacher, Turves Green School*.

Some of the more common impairments have associated voluntary organisations and many of these publish child-friendly guides to understanding the particular condition. These can be very useful to you and your child, their school or families with whom you want to share the information.

Some children will not have a 'diagnosis' because their impairment(s) may be very unusual and hard to name. They will probably be slotted under a very broad heading such as 'Global Delay' or 'learning disability'. This need not be a problem because it just means that you have to identify your child's needs from observing their behaviour and abilities, likes and dislikes. The doctors will tell you if the 'difference' is neurological, muscular, skeletal, sensory, stemming from the blood or organs, or

* From 'Snapshots of Possibility' published by the Alliance for Inclusive Education 2005

emotional, and that would be your starting point in giving an explanation, e.g. 'There is something different about your heart which makes it difficult for you to . . . '

When sharing this information with your child or others, try and avoid negative language such 'this is what is 'wrong' with you', or implying that your child is his/her impairment, e.g. 'I have a Down's child', or 'you are an epileptic'. Say instead 'you have epilepsy', or Downs Syndrome, etc. It may not seem that important, but language is very subtly powerful, helping us to form positive or negative images of ourselves.

Never Lie
It goes without saying that it is never, ever, a good thing to lie to your children in order to shield them from the imagined pain they might feel if they knew the full extent of their impairment:

"My family still tried to give me false hope – "Your sight will come back"."
Haq Ismail

I remember when I overheard my mother say to my daughter *"If you eat your greens you might be able to walk one day,"* - a statement which had not a grain of truth in it of course. I came close to matricide that afternoon, but resisted, and made do with just a tongue-lashing. If you feel tempted to make remarks like this to your child, try and find a counsellor instead and sort yourself out.

Identity and Pride

On the whole, it has to be said, disabled people have not been welcomed in most places and cultures of the world. The vast majority of people have depended on their physical strength and wit to survive and therefore being disabled would have posed a threat to their community. Little difference has been seen between sickness, impairment and madness. – they are all viewed as curses.

For most of our past our real understanding of human biology and physiology has been almost non-existent, leading to a reliance on our fears and imaginings to make sense of what happens to us. Traditionally much of this has centred on the notion of karma or punishment from the gods. To be disabled, or to give birth to a disabled child was, and sometime still is, felt to be a shameful thing. Men sometimes feel it is a reflection on their masculinity. These ideas keep a hold on us for many years after logic and evidence point to different conclusions.

Most of our impairments as human beings, in a global sense, are not forms of spiritual retribution, but are directly caused by the inequalities of the economic system, through malnutrition, lack of healthcare and hygiene, wars, exploitation at work and accidents caused by tiredness and fatigue. Even in the rich world, although the impairments are different, the main causes are still related to our way of life with depression, drug and alcohol addiction, obesity and heart disease accounting for 40% of our demands on the NHS. Only a small fraction of impairments are 'natural' and would be with us regardless of our social systems. We are not encouraged to look at this. We are encouraged to view all disability as acts of God, unfortunate and only curable by medicine and doctors, not by putting an end to poverty or greed.

It is economic inequality which makes us think there are not enough resources for everybody to live a decent life. Even in the developed world where resources are abounding, disabled people are made to feel we cost too much and somehow threaten the well being of others. We are born into a backdrop of negativity. Not only do we not get a decent welcome, but it gradually dawns on us that the State has designed and funded a system to weed us out before we are born (pre-natal screening). The best that we can then feel is that although it would have been better if we hadn't existed, now that we are here people will make the best of it.

In the past it has been worse. It appears by studying history that the powerful ruling elites of the world will stop at nothing to hold onto their positions of control and superiority. Their ability to dehumanise groups of people in order to justify the most appalling treatment of them for their own purposes, is well documented and continually shocking to acknowledge. We have seen women burnt as witches, black people bought and sold in markets like animals, working class men sent to their deaths in thousands in the name of war, homosexuals stoned to death, Jews burnt alive in giant incinerators.

Yet life moves forward, and with it our knowledge and understanding. Once, here in England, many disabled people lived in very harsh conditions in long stay hospitals and asylums, but few do now. Then, people did not see anything wrong with it. Nowadays, television images of children in similar conditions in Romania or Bulgaria cause outrage. Yet even in our rich countries in the 21st Century, some disabled people are still institutionalised, grow up without love, suffer from discrimination and are forced to live small lives. Even those who are at home in the centre of loving families still face extraordinary battles in order to be included in ordinary life as equals. It is not yet all ancient history.

The confusion we all live in is because change is slow, patchy and ultimately a personal, individual thing. Every one of us is at our own stage of learning and consequently every person you meet will hold a different attitude towards disabled people. One will be wholly negative seeing the person only in terms of the problems they might cause. Another may be wholly positive, seeing the person as a model of courage and perseverance against the odds. One parent may feel her child to be a punishment, another to feel her child to be a blessing. Professionals may hold many different views as to the best way to treat a child. Family members may hold widely different views as to how to behave towards a disabled member. Professionals will write different and often contradictory recommendations. Successive political leaders will differ on their understanding and policies. On the one hand we have the Disability Discrimination Act to protect our rights, and on the other a massive pre-natal testing service aimed at our extermination. This is deeply confusing to us all.

The worst systematic mistreatment of disabled children often begins with breaking the bond between disabled children and their parents. Once that is accomplished, the child is at the mercy of the 'State', or paid people in various forms of institutions, unprotected by love. Because it is also necessary to persuade the people who fund, manage and staff these institutions that they are doing something good, or at least inevitable, the children must never be allowed to express their true feelings, and all their suffering must be attributed to their impairments and not their treatment. This has happened in every country except, interestingly, the very poorest where families are just left to cope without help. Even in these countries however there is the danger of the West exporting our mistaken ideologies and practices through the resources, power and prestige held by large international agencies and charities.

As a result of this history, for many disabled people the struggle to feel good about ourselves is our biggest struggle. Like all oppressed or devalued groups we tend to internalise the judgements of others around us and start to believe them. We not only feel bad about ourselves but also about other members of our 'group'. This explains to some degree why disabled people who are herded together in segregated places are sometimes so horrible to each other, and it also helps to explain why we become so passive and put up with things too much, or avoid other disabled people like the plague when we grow up.

Parents are also an oppressed group with in our societies, and internalise feelings of shame and failure if we do not seem to be producing the 'right' sort of children. We are also competitive and judgemental towards other parents.

We need to be proud of ourselves as parents, even if we are not perfect, and we need to help our children have pride in their identity as disabled young people. This looks like a tricky issue for many parents.

77

Because 'disability' has been seen as such a negative thing, many well meaning allies have steered their children away from the word, and have little concept that it could be a source of pride to their children, especially as they grow into young adults.

Deaf people are particularly proud of their identity, language and community. Chris speaks about what she would have liked from her (hearing) parents as she was growing up:

"I would have liked them to know that it is not a tragedy to be deaf. It is not awful – just different and sometimes very interesting and sometimes very boring. It does not ruin your life;

I would have liked to have met some other deaf people and been encouraged to learn sign language at an early age. I would have liked the whole family to learn! I would have liked to be part of the deaf community, although I didn't want to be sent away to deaf boarding school."
Chris O'Mahony

Disabled people have other identities as well. We come from every ethnic, class and faith background, but these identities can often be ignored or distorted by the institutions around us:

"School did not help me be part of my religion or community. Asian values, ethics – disability seemed a negative thing. I was a non-person. I was 'excused' religion. I was the only Muslim in the school and there was no celebration of my religion. My Dad had been quite assertive about certain things – I was not to eat pork, no sex-education. In RE they excluded me and made me do physio instead. There was no consciousness of developing a cultural identity. I think there is a fine line between religious and cultural rules. In Islam, as far as I understand, disability is seen as a gift from God - The Key to Heaven. Life is looked upon as an endurance test. How you deal with life's pressures determines how you will be treated in the afterlife. But Pakistan is a new country, only 50 years old, and the influences from Indian culture and Hinduism are still deeply entrenched. In Hinduism disability is the result of Karma and is a very negative thing.

I think these prejudices still lie deep within my culture."
Ali Kashmiri

Haq had similar experiences in his residential school:

"I think I was the only Asian kid there. I was forced to go to chapel. The Headmaster was a Reverend but I wasn't a Christian. They made me stand up and sing. I used to mouth something else. I thought "This is not my religion" but they tried to make me fit in.

There were also issues about food. They had reassured my parents that I would get Halal food, but they made me eat such different food. My parents resorted to sending me food parcels in the post – with Articles for the Blind labels stuck on them! I received them and ate them two days later, but I never got food poisoning. I used to go into a field to eat because the students commented on the smell."
Haq Ismail

Within the medical model of course, the word 'Disability' is used as a label to describe someone as having less ability than is considered normal, as are the words 'Handicapped', 'Crippled', 'Retarded', 'Mad', etc. However, for us, trying to avoid the negativity by not acknowledging a large part of our reality is the same mistake as the 'colour blindness' we once used around skin colour for similar reasons: 'I don't think of you as black, I think of you as my friend'.

Every minority, or 'oppressed' group in society eventually has to come together to organise – to campaign for equal rights and protection under the law. It happened with women and the suffragettes, manual workers and trades unions, black people and anti-racism campaigns, the gay rights movement and it has happened with people with impairments. As we organise we begin to change the language by which we are described, sometimes inventing new words to create our own identity. One of the newest groups is DANDA who have adopted the phrase 'Neuro-Diverse' to bring together people with a number of impairments which they see as being related:

"DANDA (Developmental Adult Neuro-Diversity Association) has been set up for people with Dyspraxia, Asperger Syndrome, AD(H)D and other related conditions such as Dyslexia and Dyscalculia. It is run by adults with one or more of these conditions, thus following the Madrid declaration of 2002, which stated that organisations should be run by their users (Nothing about us without us)."
DANDA Website

Such groups all identify with the wider Disability Movement and subscribe to the 'Social Model'.

Disability Pride

PRIDE
Pride is somewhere in your soul
Pride is some place you are in control
Pride is the peace within that finally makes you whole
Celebrate your difference with pride

Pride in yourself is bound to set you free
Pride in who you are just a person like me
Pride and self-respect and gentle dignity
No one can take away your pride

Pride can make you angry. Pride can make you strong
Pride's the key that unlocks the doors to the rooms where we belong
Pride is our destiny and where we all come from
Turn around embrace your pride.

(Chorus)
Proud angry and strong.
Proud angry and strong
Proud angry and strong

Pride can make you equal without your liberty
Pride can give Its freedom to a prisoner like me

Pride is always with you wherever you may be
Once won, you'll never lose your pride

Pride is a rocky road that's straight and doesn't bend
Pride's a path you follow, pride's your closest friend
Pride's the source inside your heart from which you can draw strength
Begin all your journeyings with pride

Pride's the bond between us. Pride's the bridge we burn
Pride's the victory the battle, from which we shall return
Pride's the spark of fire within, the crucible the germ.
The seed of our power is our pride.

Lyrics by Johnny Crescendo

It is not that we are particularly proud of having impairments – that just happened to us. What we are proud of is belonging to any amazing group of people who have been feared, hated, left to die on mountain tops, called children of the devil, cut up, locked up, put in circuses, laughed at, had every human dignity taken from us, institutionalised and ignored, and we have come back to reclaim our place in the heart of our families, our communities, fought for each other, refused to be silenced, organised, become visible and demanded the right to make our contribution to the world we live in. And, as well as all that we have, for the most part, and despite such awful treatment, retained our ability to be nice people, funny, creative and good.

It is always helpful to be reminded of this when we start to feel that there really is something wrong with us. Your child (and you, if you are a disabled parent) needs not only to feel good about themselves, but good about disabled people as a whole. It is not helpful to teach us to compare ourselves with other disabled people, e.g. 'At least you don't have a learning disability' or 'at least you are not in a wheelchair'. In fact it helps none of us to feel good about ourselves only because we feel better than someone else, nor of course, does it follow that we should feel bad about ourselves because there are people more able than us.

Over the last forty years a collective, self-organised movement has been formed to represent the views and demands of people with physical, sensory, intellectual and emotional impairments. To do this we had to overcome these internalised feelings and rebuild our relationships with each other based on respect and common goals. In so doing we reconnected with the truth about ourselves – that we are fine, worthy people deserving of a decent life, equal rights and a valued place in the world. It was very liberating for us. This movement created the medical and social model framework to understand how our particular inequalities are framed and justified. It reclaimed the label of 'disabled people' to mean that we identify collectively as a group of people who are discriminated against by society because we have impairments. This is a powerful thing. Our collective voice has brought about big changes from which you and your child are now benefiting - The Disability Living Allowance; Direct Payments; accessible transport; the Disability Discrimination Act, to name but a few. This movement is still largely invisible within society and, therefore, also from up and coming generations of young people and their parents.

This book is not a chronicle of the Rise of the Disability Movement, but is a call to parents to find out about it. (See back of book for info). You cannot force the identity on your child, and nor should you, but you can help them discover the existence off local self-advocacy groups, young physical people's forums, videos, books and films about our movement. Edwina and Jackie remind us of the importance of role models for young disabled people:

"It was meeting disabled people who had a bigger life who showed me that things were possible."
Edwina Macarthy

"I got a job at Lambeth Accord in 1990 and my life really began then. I discovered the disability movement and understood the injustice given to disabled people. I discovered People First (the self-advocacy movement of people with learning difficulties) and disabled people who were radical campaigners."
Jackie Downer MBE

From these resources they will get access to the information about the medical and social models which, for many young people is a hugely liberating perspective. It is the place where their real pride can be born.:

"I discovered the Social Model of disability at age 30 at the Greenwich Association of Disabled People. It turned my life around. Until then I thought I was a nuisance."
John Ley

Friendship is Fundamental

Once people mostly lived in tribes or big families connected to other big families in villages. Children were seen as a collective responsibility. Now it is not uncommon for a sole parent to be the only responsible adult in a child's life. This is not good. It doesn't work for any family and it especially doesn't work if you or your child are having problems.

Family members are still very important, especially grandparents who are responsible for 50% of the childcare in the UK, but they are still not enough. We all need friends. You need friends. Your children need friends.

Although it is true that we live very busy lives, it is also true that most people like to feel useful and to learn about new things. Some of you will already have friends who are sticking by you as you learn how to support your child(ren), and they are to be treasured. Some of you will find that you need to build some new relationships with perhaps a completely different set of people, because your priorities and interests will have been changed by being the parent of a disabled child.

Your child also needs friends. There is no child however serious or whatever the nature of their impairment, who does not need friends. This is true for children who cannot speak or move voluntarily, it is true of children with emotional issues, and it is true of children with autism, whatever the professionals say.

What is a friend? We all have our own answers. Someone who likes being with you; someone who makes you feel safe; someone who makes you laugh; someone who shares your interests/obsessions; someone who continues to think about you when you are not together; someone who will help you when you need it; someone you trust and who trusts you. Friendship can happen between people with greatly different backgrounds or abilities.

Some of the friendships which can now develop between disabled and non-disabled young people because of inclusive settings have amazed the adults around them. William is a child with cerebral palsy and no speech. Natasha is a non-disabled classmate in a mainstream primary school in Brighton which William attends three days a week in preparation for his full-time inclusion. This quote is from Natasha's mother:

"William has been fantastic for Natasha. She began by being frightened of him, but now he is one of her closest friends. She now understands that he is not threat, just has different needs. It has helped her self-esteem and confidence. She is more sparkly when she knows William will be in school. She gets up and says 'It's a William day today'. She never wants to miss school when he is there, even when she is ill. They have a special friendship."*

Because of the history of separation, when a child (or adult) has a significant impairment, just getting children together in the same room, or 'integrated' class, may not always be enough. Children may have 'caught' the sense of 'otherness' from the adults around them, may be wary, or may think that the disabled child needs adults around them all the time instead of other children. It is possible they may be nervous of unusual sounds or movements or behaviours and decide to stay away from them. Or in the case where the child's impairments are not visible, but their behaviour is 'odd', other children may feel pulled to project their own bad feelings onto the child, to victimise them or bully them. This must not be ignored or denied. It takes conscious action on the part of teachers, support staff and parents to help the children to make positive connections with each other.

Disabled children in segregated schools may also mistreat each other, and have an additional problem in that it is often impossible for them to facilitate each other, making constant adult support and supervision a necessity and therefore close friendships hard to make. The long journeys many such children have to make each day, taking them away from their local communities, and their specific needs for access or support often means that playing after school, or sleepovers in each other's houses just don't happen.

* From 'Snapshots of Possibility' published by the Alliance for Inclusive Education 2005

"I had no friends at home. My brothers and sisters went out having fun but I stayed at home with Mum watching TV. TV was my lifeline, and playing by myself. I would have loved to have my school friends over but our parents did not meet or network and we couldn't write down each other's phone numbers and organise things ourselves. It just never happened."
Jackie Downer MBE

For many disabled children, having friends who are not similarly disabled is the only way they can enter the young people's community around them, have fun, take risks and be naughty, just like everyone else. - a vital part of growing up. This is not to say we don't also need and treasure friendships with other disabled young people, and adults in later life.

Many of us who are parents of disabled children have to think about how to set up situations in which our disabled children can be free to play without constant adult supervision. Memories of this sort of free play are often our happiest. This could mean playing on their own, but it should also mean with other children who are at least partially able to enable your disabled child to join in. For this to happen you might have to learn how to tell other children about your child's impairments and needs, especially if your child is unable to do so for themselves. When my daughter was very young for example, in any situation with new people I had to start by making a kind of public announcement. I had to say that there was a child in the room who had very brittle bones and that this meant they must not pick her up without asking me first, sit on her, knock her over or throw heavy things at her, and if she suddenly started screaming, they were not to move her but to call me. As she got older I was amazed at how competent her friends became at helping her move around safely, and even how to deal with the technicalities of her powered wheelchair. They also knew very clearly when they needed adult assistance and would ask for it. My role was mainly to hang around being 'on call', providing crisps and juice on demand.

Some children will be happy to learn skills, such as giving your child a drink, using Makaton or British Sign Language, or guiding a blind child. We have found many children are better at understanding children with speech impairments than adults, and they will often become their 'interpreters'. However they cannot learn these things if no one trusts them enough to try.

Because many of us parents are not in full time work because of the extra 'duties' we have, we have found ourselves becoming a sort of community resource for young people, being more available than most parents who are working as well as raising their family. It is likely too that if our child has a physical impairment, then our house will be the one which is accessible and child-friendly. It used to upset me that children came often to our house but my daughter did not in return receive many invitations to play at their houses. I started thinking that maybe the children did not really like her or want to play with her, but I soon realised it was the parents who had the difficulties. They did not have the time or attention to support their child's play times in the ways which were needed if a significantly disabled child, such as mine, was to be included. I decided to accept it as a fact of life and get on with being the unofficial playgroup down the road. I then became a refuge for some children who were very neglected and this taught us all a very important lesson. My daughter was not the most needy child around. She was needed too.

As children grow older they reflect their membership of their friendship group by the clothes they wear, hairstyles and choice of music. As many cash-struck parents know this can be an expensive and annoying pressure on us to buy the right trainers, schoolbags etc. But if your child is dependent on you to dress them, do their hair and buy their things and you want to help them feel they are 'one of the gang', then it is really important that you find out what is 'cool' for the group your child seems most comfortable in, and help them have the necessary gear. Better still, let them go shopping with their friends and prepare to be a normal, broke and disapproving parent as a result.

Circles of Support

There are some organisations which have recognised the fundamental need for connection and friendship between disabled children and their peers, and that sometimes the family, or school, or both, may need extra help to make this happen. The most common 'tool' used by these organisations is the Circle of Support. The essence of this is that an outside person, or 'ally' takes on the role of bringing together a number of people who are willing to think about how the 'focus' person can be supported to have a full life, despite any labels or difficulties. Circles can happen at school, or at home, or wherever the person is living. Members usually commit themselves to stick around for a while, sometimes years. *(More about Circles can be found at the back of this book).* The people who developed these tools saw that we are all suffering in the modern world from a breakdown of community. They believe that we now have to intentionally create new communities around ourselves if we are not to be overwhelmed with isolation and loneliness. All members of a circle benefit, not just the focus person, because it brings people together and provides the opportunity for them to connect in meaningful ways and for useful purposes.

Maureen talks about the importance to her of the Circle of Support which she has created for her son Aaron. Aaron is now nineteen and has autism. He is non-verbal and uses Makaton to communicate. Aaron has had a big struggle to be included in mainstream education which he has now left. He is using his circle to help plan his adult life:

"Aaron's current Circle of Support started 2 years ago, as part of my recovery from being deeply wounded by all the negativity that had come out of the fight for Aaron's inclusion and the knowledge that he was never able to fully experience inclusion at school. For over a year after our final tribunal hearing I remained in what felt like a very lonely and painful place made worse by the fact of Aaron being incarcerated in an institution and environment that so obviously failed to meet the needs of all who attended, worked or sent their children there.

Faced with the problem of being so spiritually depleted and physically and mentally exhausted the only way forward seemed to take some time to reconnect with myself and my goals. I needed to call on others to look out for Aaron whilst I met more of my own needs and so I called on friends, old and new, to form a Circle of support for Aaron. But as he no longer had any peers to enrol it was mostly my friends who formed the Circle.

This time these Circle members have brought more energy and even more hope than the first Circle Aaron had. The previous Circle was a totally new experience and some participants attended as a favour but few were really willing to take action to positively affect changes for Aaron.

*This time I had the benefit of having participated myself in someone else's Circle and from this experience realised how **very difficult** and yet **extremely important** establishing and being part of a Circle, can be.*

I went on the Inclusive Solutions website and purchased 2 titles which I felt were essential tools to use in providing shape and structure for myself and everyone who unlike me may have never previously known of Circles.

The Circle has consistently tried to meet every 6 weeks and has grown to 10 committed members who attend regularly or offer support in other ways. And new members are always welcome and welcomed.

For the Circle anyone joining at any stage can at a glance, see & know what is going on for Aaron. And to make the Circle accessible to Aaron, the original copies of the PATH has symbols and illustrations and Makaton signing is used during Circle activities.

The whole process is 'Aaron-centred' i.e. enabling and facilitating his contributions and choices, and his attendance is encouraged (but cannot be insisted onJ). However the circle is always looking at ways to enhance Aaron's involvement in decisions which directly and indirectly affect and influence his life. Helpful new suggestions and ideas are always welcomed".

Two years on, Aaron has a PATH and a MAP which relate to his transition from schoolboy to adulthood. These are both methods of life planning using person-centred principles. *(See 'Useful Publications' at the end of the book for more information).* Maureen continues:

"We have now developed the function of Circle activities to be even more inclusive and to focus on future planning of Aaron's adult life. To help us with this, Aaron frequently takes Circle members by bus & underground, out to some of his favourite haunts. Although the destination is always a surprise, increasingly Aaron's knowledge of London and skilful use of public transport is no longer surprising.

As a Circle we also hire a minibus for days out or arrange a Circle 'taxi' for clubbing etc! Jean our excellent volunteer coordinator sends regular emails of Circle dates and 'training' to keep members up to date with the purpose and value to all of us of Circle activities.

The future is uncertain but we have plans! Although amongst us we have many amazing talents, we are looking towards developing a Circle of people much closer to Aaron in age, outlook and experiences. This is reflected in the current MAP which we as a Circle have drawn up to enable Aaron to be 'In Control' of his future.

What having a Circle for Aaron means to me is, to paraphrase another Circle member; it allows "Aaron to be Aaron". But it also allows me to be me and others to be themselves. It does this by adding so much good and focussing consciously and unconsciously on being bigger than the limitations of our single selves. When the Circle is activated in, around, and including Aaron, it shatters so many of the illusions and prejudices of this society that it is truly a powerful and wonderful thing. Yet it is what non-disabled people and their non-disabled peers, siblings, families, friends and communities can take for granted.

Aaron has provided us all opportunities to be so much bigger people. To see the world through far more creative and inventive eyes and use our imaginations to experience possibilities many would consider impossible.

Aaron everyday without fail, expresses his love and appreciation to all who are aware and able to see it and I have a feeling that everyone who contributes to the circle are proud of Aaron and of ourselves and are determined to not be defeated. But instead to keep on making necessary

efforts for change and for equal rights to happiness!"
Maureen Johnson

Fayon, one of the circle members has this to say about how much she gets from being part of the group:

"I have known Aaron and Maureen for around 7 years now and I have been involved in Aarons circle for a couple of years. The reason I like to contribute is because I feel it is important for Aaron to have a variety of friends around him. Aaron is the only autistic person who I know so I learn a lot about his life by spending time with him. As I love to go out and enjoy myself, I like to support Aaron the best way I can so that he can have access to the same social nightlife (or as close as we can) as other 19/20 year olds. Why should he miss out on dancing and music? He is friendly, fun and a really cool guy! We have already been clubbing and we really enjoyed ourselves. I look forward to our next night out."
Fayon Cottrell

Include Yourself

As well as thinking about your child's lack of friends, examine your own social circle. Think abut the role of friends in your own life, both in the past and now. Is there anyone outside of your family or paid professionals that you trust and talk to about important things. Do you spend time with them, have fun with them or pursue common hobbies and interests. If the answer to this is no, then you have identified the first problem which needs solving. Modelling isolation and loneliness will not help either you or your child(ren). Many of us feel enormous guilt when we think of the apparent sacrifices our parents made giving us a good life. Rosaleen spells it out:

"Just when my parents got to the time in their lives when they could worry a little less about me, go on holidays more, enjoy their hobbies and spend more time together, my mother passed away.

By this time I was happily married, holding down a full-time job and had PAs (personal assistants) to help me with my personal requirements.

Although my parents were always there and always would act as a safety net or come running to help if requested, it was no longer something they had to consider 24 hours a day seven days a week.

It breaks my heart that they never got the chance of freedom, the time to take the opportunities to do things as and when they wanted, spontaneously and on a whim.

So, remember that despite the love and devotion that you will have for your disabled child, remember that you have a life to live also. Make provision for that whilst you are still supporting your disabled child -- don't leave it too late."
Rosaleen Moriarty-Simmonds

Getting A Rest

Parenting is the most challenging and relentless job that anyone does. All children are born totally dependant on adults and in need of 24 hour care. This comes as a great shock to many a first time mother or father. All your routines have to change to accommodate the needs of another including when you eat and how much you sleep. Because this is all considered normal in our societies, we have developed many natural supports for parents and for young people, right through to adulthood.

These start often with members of our close family moving in with us, or visiting more often in order to help with the new baby. As the baby grows a little older we employ babysitters to allow us to go out and have some relaxing time with our partners, family or friends. Those of us with more financial resources may pay for a live-in Au Pair or Nanny to help with household chores and childcare.

If we need to return to work we can chose between a number of childcare services, including grandparents (grandparents provide 50% of all childcare in the UK). As our children grow older the great State Baby Sitting Service called the education system offers us time in every weekday and eventually Big School to give us a break. Schools are now offering extended services such as after-school clubs and holiday play schemes as they become increasingly geared to the notion of supporting parents to work full time in paid jobs, (as well as their full time voluntary job of parenting.)

In addition to these supports, there are many opportunities for young people to pursue activities outside of the family home, ranging from playing in friends houses, 'sleep overs', joining youth clubs, Scouts, Brownies or Woodcraft Folk, going to classes to learn extra things like drama, music, joining in sports events such as local football teams, or singing with a choir. There is the underestimated role of 'hanging out' with friends and practicing romance, all requiring the lack of adult supervision to work. It is this rich array of choices and opportunities which makes parenting a pleasurable, or at least manageable activity for most families, both adults and children.

The problem for many families whose child(ren) are disabled, chronically ill, have learning difficulties or behaviour which challenges social 'norms' is that many of these natural supports appear closed off, or inappropriate. Children become bored and frustrated and adults become exhausted. The parents' natural supports are also lost, especially for mothers who typically give up their paid work in order to care for their child. They lose money, and they lose status, and they lose the connection with their colleagues and friends at work. The situation can get desperate.

At this point Services are called in and expected to help. The problem is that many of these services are based on the medical model, offering 'solutions' that identify the disabled child as the problem, claiming that their special needs are putting an unbearable burden on the family. Special (segregated) provision and respite care are seen as ways to give the carers a 'break' whilst at the same time being able to trust that the child's needs will be met.

When I was a child, there was no such thing as respite care. I am glad. If my parents had even suggested such a thing to me, I would never have forgiven them. A common thread amongst many of the contributions written for this book was the appreciation of our parent's determination to protect the normality of family life. Like many people, memories of our family holidays in particular remain bright spots in what may well have been difficult times:

"Despite their hardships my parents were determined that we would have 'as normal a life as possible'. We always went away for summer holidays – camping as they couldn't afford posh holidays in hotels. This must have been quite a feat with two disabled youngsters, two wheelchairs, camping equipment in an Austin A34 van. Each year as mum bought more and more camping equipment the van got lower and lower on its springs until it almost scraped its way to Scotland, the Lake District or Cornwall or other far flung places in the British Isles, bulging at the seams."
Mary Harrison

"We would go camping, I would break something, we would go to hospital and either carry on with the holiday or come home – but there are certainly hours and hours of home movies of us all having fun."
Wilma Lawrie

Compare this to Dave Morris's account of the intervention of Social Services soon after his impairment was diagnosed:

"It is strange, but suddenly the concept of family holiday ended. At seven we are all still dependent; we still need the personal assistance of our parents. But somehow we disabled children become burdensome. A regular visitor from some Christian children's organisation clearly gave this message and arrangements were made to send me away to Lancing in Sussex. A house with donkeys and a private beach and a nice name that I cannot remember. A house run by nuns.

The social worker wanted to send me away there and then. Wrap me up and pack me into an ambulance and wave goodbye. Out of sight and out of mind and let the family holiday continue without me. However, my father had a problem with religion. The son of a strict Methodist lay preacher, my father had a healthy disregard for the Lord's messengers on earth combined with a stratum of guilt. I was the result of past sin without a doubt, but no son of his would-be dispatched anywhere without checking up first. So we went down to Lancing for a visit to reassure and assuage the guilt. We turned up without notice. The head nun did not want to let us in. It simply was not done. My father would not take no for an answer. Thank God for that!

I am told that I refused to speak to my mother for a week after the visit. A week is a very long time when you are seven. I suppose that the visit was very short. It remains with me, however, as if it were a visit to hell. I remember biscuits were being baked and cooling on a table in a corridor. Opposite a whole line of toilets; doors open, old people straining and moaning; shadows of people, soulless and hopeless looking on at a small boy. A smell like nothing else. We were shown the play area. Stark and empty, one small battered teddy bear was on the floor. There was nothing

else just a barred window and heavy iron barred door with a heavy stiff and rusted lock. The final straw was the fact that the guiding nun found it difficult to open the door. We left never to return. I went on the family holiday for the last time."
Dave Morris

Renaming Respite Care as 'Short Breaks' does not make this concept any less offensive to disabled people. A break from what? And to us, nearly all provision which is in institutional settings such as old people's homes, children's wards, children's homes or even purpose built centres are all forms of segregation – a relic of the past. And yet, a real problem remains – children are bored and parents exhausted.

The 'social model' identifies the problem as the barriers preventing access to the natural resources available to non-disabled children. To this end there are new ways being developed to broaden out family support for even children with very high-level support needs. All these have a long-term goal of community development. Included in this list are home based supports such as specialist childminders, not afraid to be left alone with a disabled child because they have been given training to meet their extra needs, and children's support workers or Personal Assistants, chosen by the family and paid for by Social Services under the Direct Payments Scheme. This kind of provision brings the much needed extra pair of hands into the family home to help with care needs, play with the children, take the children out to local activities, accompany the family on holiday or whatever the family decides to is useful support. Some families employ teams of PA's, to help provide 24 hour support when previously a residential placement may have been the only option.

Moving out of the family home, Shared Care schemes usually consist of local families who have put themselves forward to offer their home to a disabled child to visit on a regular basis. The schemes support both families by matching them up and providing information, advice and a listening ear to help the arrangement to work. Some provide financial assistance to the link family so that poorer people can be involved.

Access to inclusive services in the mainstream is now a right for disabled children. Under the Disability Discrimination Act, all providers have to ensure they do not prevent a disabled person using their services or provide those services in such a way as to be offering them less favourable treatment. All services have to make 'reasonable adjustments' before they can claim that they cannot meet the needs of a disabled client. This can include one-to-one support and training for their whole staff. Physical access is also being built in or improved in many childcare centres, nurseries and schools.

It is only by being part of these mainstream communities that other 'natural' supports become available - your child will have contact with other children. They may make friends. Your child may want to go and visit their friend or go out with them to McDonalds or the playground. You may take them and meet their parents. You may make friends. You may ask them all over to tea. Their child may belong to the local Brownie Pack which is trying to be inclusive. They may offer to take your child as well as their own. Their child will be having a birthday party soon and they will feel confident enough that they can invite your disabled child to come and stay the night. You say you could not bring them or stay with them because of your other children, but you could ask the child's PA to come with them. A supported 'ordinary' life begins to happen. Your child is not so isolated and bored. You are not so isolated and tired, and, most importantly, your child remains secure in the family and begins to feel they are a valued member of their local community with the right to be included. In the long term our concept of a 'normal' community will expand to include the full diversity of humanity who live within it.

Of course, 'ordinary' life is not always an easy life. One thing I learned as a parent of a disabled child is that many 'typical' families struggle to manage. I became aware of a level of 'natural' supports which seems almost unrecognized. As young people grow older they are more able to choose where to go, who to go with, who supports them. When their own families cannot give them what they need, it is possible for them to simply move out and go and live with someone else, if the 'someone else' is willing to have them. I myself have offered this sort of refuge to some of my daughter's friends at times when they needed it. This is also true of other families I know. Two such host families eventually became official foster carers, but mostly it was something informally done and unrecorded. Because of that it is probably much more common than is recognized. What struck me about these informal arrangements is that they were all initiated by the young people. They did the choosing. Mostly the intervention helped the situation, and mostly they returned home weeks, months, or years later and rebuilt the relationship with their parents, many of whom were suffering from mental health difficulties or addictions. What also struck me was how there was nowhere for us 'refuge providers' to get any help, even with such basic things as paying for their food.

When children choose their support, it is often based firstly on a peer relationship, e.g. a friend, or cousin and secondly on their associated adults. As all our services become more 'person-centred' or 'child centred', it seems to me that we need to build in a great deal of flexibility so that the child's own relationships can be supported rather than just those of the adults.

The Big Inclusion Debate

One of the questions we often still hear is 'Does inclusion work?' or 'Can it work for everyone?' This is often coming from parents who have tried enrolling their disabled child in a mainstream school and found varying levels of hostility, reluctance and ignorance on the part of the staff and governors. Their child has become unhappy, or the school has suggested they would be better placed elsewhere. In the face of these experiences, the question is a valid one.

Disabled people however come at this question from our own viewpoint. Many of us have experienced segregation and exclusion as children and we are here to tell you it does not work. It may be that our special schools were safe and protective. A few of us even got a good education in them, although most did not, especially if you had been labelled as having learning difficulties:

"Our school was next door to an ordinary secondary school. They called us the Backwards School and did not want to know us. I used to hide from them. The work was very limited – woodwork, maths, English, cooking, PE, woodwork, maths, English, cooking, PE, woodwork and on and on. We didn't take exams. College was just like school, special classes and the same lessons. We did sit in the canteen with the other students but they didn't want to sit with us.

I don't think they want you to overlearn things in special school. They want you to achieve a bit, but not too much or they will be out of a job and their mortgages on their pretty cottages in Cornwall will not get paid"
Jackie Downer MBE

Many of us have good memories of friends we made which have lasted a lifetime. None of this however makes up for the long-term damage done by our removal from ordinary life, preventing us, or our non-disabled peers from learning how to live together in the real world:

"The effect of being sent to a special boarding school affected me in a number of ways, the first mentioned earlier was that I became unable to show emotion in public. Secondly, most of my childhood was spent in a state of fear and apprehension. That first parting from my parents ingrained in me the fact that losing people and home is incredibly difficult. I think this is called 'separation complex'. I've always found it difficult to lose people - manifested by hanging onto inappropriate boyfriends and being 'dumped' always felt like the end of the world.

Thirdly, I developed a food fear as a result of traumatic dinner times at that first school. I have awful memories of being forced to eat mashed potato (which I hated) as well as witnessing other children being force-fed and various other mealtime abuses. It's not that it happened once, but it happened every day, and as a result the food phobia developed. As an adult I had a phobia of eating in restaurants and 'special occasion' type meals, although this did not develop into full blown anorexia nervosa. It led to numerous embarrassing and awkward social situations, too numerous to go into here. I took me years to get to grips with this problem, but I did eventually.

Fourthly, when I finally left school and emerged into the real world, it was a huge culture shock. Part of me felt like a butterfly emerging from a cocoon, albeit a not very nice cocoon, but at the same time that butterfly felt very lonely and an oddity emerging into a hostile world full of able-bodied people who had very little experience of seeing wheelchair users. The butterfly had left all its other cocoon friends and cocoon world behind. It took a great adjustment. Being in an all disabled environment does not really prepare you for the real world, and of course the 'real world' is not prepared for you."
Mary Harrison

"The experience of being hidden away, with the assumption that I was worthless, still haunts me with a terror I can't describe. Nobody should be put through that. Yet there are hundreds forcibly excluded from life everyday."
Maresa Mackeith

For those of us who lived one or two generations ago, there was little choice for parents. Like me, Wilma was refused entry into mainstream education for fear of her 'fragility':

"Despite having many fractures during my childhood, my parents always allowed me to play outside with my friends or they came to me when leg fractures meant time in bed, and when it came time for me to start school, my mum took me to the local primary school to register me to begin in August. That was when they realised that my life would be very different than my big brother, Brian (he's 10 years older than me). The school refused to accept me because of the risks (this was in 1965), they then tried to enrol me in a girl's private school - my brother went to one for boys in the centre of town. I remember sitting in the car with him waiting for them to come back to tell me I'd be starting soon, but no. Again, it was 'too risky' and they were told to take me to a 'special' school. At that time there weren't the supports or organisations like the Alliance for Inclusive Education or Parents for Inclusion or other disabled role models to give the guidance to change perceptions and raise understanding. So that was me, caught up in the continuum of medical services and consigned to segregated provision, but in my heart I always missed going to school with my local pals."
Wilma Lawrie

Haq tells of his experience as a young boy with a visual impairment in the 1980's:

"There was no choice about my secondary education – home or Worcester College. Both seem abhorrent. I didn't want to go to Boarding School. "Go and have a look" the LEA said, and arranged a taxi. I felt sick to the stomach. The day I went my Mum made me my favourite food and I threw up on the way. It was the only way to protest - the only way to say "Don't force me".

Worcester felt like a hospital. There was a clinical smell. It was cold. Blind people looked like aliens to me. I said "I'm not coming here." "Don't worry" said the cheery teachers – "You'll be so welcome. Football pitch,

Swimming pool. We are all a big family here." It was in an idyllic setting. I didn't buy it.

I had to do the entrance exam. Maths was difficult but English easy. I still said that I was not going to Worcester. I passed. I still didn't want to go. I had tantrums. My Parents were resigned to the fact. They didn't know what else to do. They put it off till January and I was home for my brothers wedding. Time passed and finally I had to go. I couldn't sleep the night before. It felt that the whole world was crashing round me. We packed all sorts of things. Name tags. 4 shirts. 3 trousers. Very regimented.

There were big smiles from the staff on arrival. I couldn't let go of my Dad. The whole place seemed so cold. Because of my delayed start the others had been there 3 months already and had made friends. The routines were already set.

The House Parents had their own favourites. Some got cuddled. I didn't feel loved there. They changed when our parents came and gave the impression that everyone was looked after equally, when in fact there was a clear difference in the way that pupils were treated."
Haq Ismail

"My mother recently told me the difficulties my parents had had getting a local school for Phil (who was three years older than me). None of the immediate local schools would take him because of his disability. She must have lost a lot of confidence being refused by so many schools. Eventually they found a very small one teacher school who ran her outfit from her living room and she agreed to take him. This school was two miles away and did not provide lunch for the 12 children that attended. My mother had to take him on the bus or walk (with me in tow as a baby) to this school, collect him again to bring him home for lunch, and then back to school again for the afternoon and then again to bring him home. My parents couldn't afford a car at that time. This exhausting arrangement continued for a year apparently until social services stepped in and persuaded mum and dad to send him to a special boarding school for disabled children, the Victoria Home for Crippled Children. I followed three years later. Mum has repeatedly told me how painful it was to leave us at boarding school

and is quite haunted by it. She had to immerse herself in something to take her mind off the situation and subsequently went to teacher training college and became a mathematics teacher. My mother brings up the subject of our early schooling often and I find myself constantly reassuring her that she did the right thing, or rather the ONLY thing. It's only recently that I realise how the lack of local schools at that time adversely affected myself and my whole family."
Mary Harrison

Rosaleen also speaks of the lack of choice facing her and her family:

"Education is the foundation to your child's future. Based on my own experience of education both in 'special education in schools' and 'mainstream education' I can categorically say that I learned more in the inclusive mainstream schools than anywhere. My parents wanted me to go into mainstream education from the outset, but during the 1960s it was virtually unheard of for a wheelchair user to attend mainstream schools. The local authority would not allow it and consequently I ended up in a 'special school' -- I learned hardly anything in the first 10 years of my academic journey. My parents kept fighting and eventually I did manage to get into a school for disabled people that actually gave disabled people an education. I then went on to a college for disabled people. But I only truly appreciated that at last I was on par with my non-disabled peers when finally I was accepted into a mainstream college, followed by university. Being accepted there is one thing, and I quickly learned that I had to sink or swim by my own means. Because I was so grateful for having been given this opportunity I was too afraid to ask for too much assistance -- this would have reinforced any fears that the pessimists within the organisation had about disabled people being a 'problem' and causing the organisation insurmountable hassle.

Thankfully things have changed and your children now have a right to go to mainstream schools, and a right to support, to enable them to thrive there. Do make sure that your child exercises their right to a meaningful and worthwhile education."
Rosaleen Moriarty-Simmonds

Many non-disabled people fondly imagine that bullying only happens in mainstream schools. They believe that because all the children in segregated schools are 'in the same boat' they will be full of support and empathy for each other. Dream on. Bullying is endemic in special schools, based on a hierarchy of type or severity of impairment, with physical impairment-but walking at the top, and learning difficulty-without- speech at the bottom, and it is made worse because no one sees it:

"We had four mixed ability classes each covering a four-year age range, from 5 years to 16. I was completely bored stiff by the age of 10. Learning stopped and I really got angry with the other children who I blamed for being 'thick'. I had one gorgeous friend who I felt was my intellectual equal, but she had a hole in the heart and died at 13. I was left alone with people I was told were 'autistic'. I spent all my time changing their routines to upset them. I remember persuading one boy, Mark Masters, to throw some tennis shoes, which belonged to a teacher I hated, into a stream. The teacher went berserk. Mark turned pale and fainted with fright. I was his biggest tormentor. I am ashamed of that now, but not then. I was fuelled by anger and boredom."
Jane Campbell

Ali has similar memories:

"I was bullied as a child and then I became a bully. I remember one child who used to do these painful 'Chinese burns' on me. One day, when I had just got a new powered wheelchair, a spark of anger suddenly rose up within me and I used the chair to tip him out of his. I got into trouble because he had spina bifida and hydrocephalus. He had a shunt in his head and they told me I could have killed him. I was labelled as someone not to go near. It made me feel very powerful. I became King amongst the other young people. I had 30 of them under my thumb. There was a hierarchy of impairment at school. People who were incontinent and 'smelly' were at the bottom. I remember being asked to help to 'get so and so'. I used manipulation to get him into a classroom where the others were all waiting to beat him up. It was a way to vent my anger".
Ali Kashmiri

Ali believes these experiences as children are long lasting and contribute to a difficulty many disabled people face when we are adults – being harsh and competitive towards each other, sometimes being the victim, sometimes the perpetrator:

"This goes on onto adulthood. Disabled people can treat each other very badly. Now I have gone back to feeling vulnerable and allowing disabled people to put me down. I need to stay away from most of them. I can only deal with people who have risen above this. Frustration can make me arrogant or they control me. It seems it has to be one or the other. It goes back to our childhood. We are very judgmental of each other. The hierarchy is still there. Disabled people with speech impairments are ignored, including by other disabled people."
Ali Kashmiri

Haq remembers his unhappiness at Worcester College:

"There was lots of psychological bullying. The first three or four years were hell for me. I cried myself to sleep every night."
Haq Ismail

Mary remembers how it was for her brother at the Shaftesbury Society School:

"Phil was in the top stream and was quite bullied by the more able bodied boys. There were no electric wheelchairs then and the most severely disabled had to wait for other boys or staff to push them around in their manual wheelchairs."
Mary Harrison

Sending a child down this route is often the start of a separate life, reaching into adulthood. This is because the medical model itself (unless a cure is found) does not work. Gallons of speech therapy, physiotherapy, high staff ratios and narrowed curriculum will do nothing in the end to prepare your child for full, self-directed life in the community. Most will go on to 'discrete' (segregated) courses at FE colleges, sheltered employment or to languishing in a 'Day Wasting Centre'. Some will do better than that, perhaps going on to university and leaving home to live in a flat with support. But the isolation, undeveloped social skills, loss of a young community to belong to, insecurity around relationships, is likely to be a very long lasting emotional and social legacy at that early separation. Wilma speaks of how much she had to learn about 'ordinary life' when she finally made it into mainstream education as a trainee teacher:

"During my post grad year in teacher training, we all had to do three placements in schools. My first day of teaching practice as a fresh faced student teacher was surprising in ways I had not even considered - not the excitement of putting into practice all that we had been learning, nor the thought of getting to know all of my 'pupils' as individuals, nor the challenge of making my lessons clear and interesting for them, nor the enormous responsibility of my future career.

What brought me to a metaphorical standstill was realising, as the Head of Department left the classroom to take a phone call leaving me with her 25 third year accounting pupils ("If you have any questions, Miss Lawrie will answer them"), that this was the first time in my 20 years on the planet, that I had been in a classroom with more than 6 pupils and they were all about the same age! They all looked to me as the person who knew everything. I looked to them as the ones who were going to teach me what life in mainstream school was like - my learning curve was HUGE, almost a vertical line."
Wilma Lawrie

Of course for some young people, especially those in residential provision from a young age, the outcome is likely to be a lifetime of institutional living.

So what does a caring parent do when mainstream doesn't seem to be a possibility? Firstly, remember that there isn't a wonderful alternative called 'Special School' because of all the reasons above. Bullying and exclusions happen in special schools too, apart from the narrow educational opportunities offered within them.

Secondly, ask yourself if what you are hoping for is medical model type provision in the mainstream, e.g. lots of speech therapy. If that is the case then you will probably be disappointed. The move to educate disabled children in mainstream schools is a move towards the social model, prioritising friendships, a wider choice of curriculum, better teachers, the development of social skills and a sense of belonging. It is also aimed at fostering real connections between young people from all manner of diverse backgrounds and cultures, so that the prejudices of the past can be dissolved by real knowledge and empathy. Some therapy will also be available, but it will probably not take the major role it might in segregated provision.

What many parents and children have experienced in mainstream schools is not 'inclusion' at all. Inclusion is a long-term goal which has to be fought for.

Most Local Authorities are still practicing 'integration' which means putting the most able disabled children in unchanged mainstream schools with a small amount of extra help, adaptations or equipment, with the expectation that they will probably do better academically than they would in a special school.

One of the difficulties of these policies is for the children left behind in the shrinking special school population. Sapna speaks of her experience:

"I am looking back to the time I went to a special school and consider the influence and effects it had on me then and now.
M--- School, what did it mean to be there for me? Why did I have so many problems there? How did it affect me mentally, physically and emotionally? I was in an unnatural environment, I think due to my speech impairment, I could not prove myself to the teachers; I didn't have communication skills because some of the other kids had learning disabilities. The teachers did not realise that I could actually speak and my brain was in full working order. Even though I would communicate with my family and friends, the teachers would not encourage me to communicate verbally with them and I was too young to understand that I had a greater potential than they

realised. I communicated by pointing to 'makaton' signs on a board (a form of visual sign language). I soon found this was a frustrating way to communicate since there was a limit to how much I could say. However I learnt to read the words underneath and did not bother to learn the large number of the signs.

Gradually there was a decline in the level of education. The school was left with fewer children who had severe mental and physical disabilities. After this time, there were fewer subjects and the work became a lot less challenging. This is when I noticed that I was deteriorating mentally and it was extremely frightening even though it was a gradual process. By now most of the reasonably good or better teachers had left and the school was employing those with little or no experience with disability and with very low expectations of those who they supposedly taught. I am not sure of the time scale but my mental deterioration due to the lack of stimulation meant that I was no longer able to do the same kind of work that I was previously capable of. It was extremely frightening and I did not have the vocabulary to express my extreme frustration.

The teachers never found out that I had the ability to read and write which I only managed to learn extensively at the age of seventeen, when I was placed in a mainstream school.

I think that what parents need to learn is that children cannot be segregated into special needs and mainstream schools, this is just fundamentally wrong, no matter how severely disabled they are."
Sapna Ramnani

An inclusive school is one which recognises the 'whole' child, whoever they are, and takes responsibility for creating a learning environment in which they can feel safe, known and valued. If a child is having difficulties they are assumed to be because the institution is not answering their needs rather than finding the fault in the child.

It will help to know your rights. Children have few rights in the world, and disabled children even less, but they do now have some. The most significant is the Disability Discrimination Act. This law requires all service providers, including nurseries, schools and colleges, to change their practice through 'reasonable adjustments'; to make their service available to disabled people. This includes children, parents, employees (such as teachers) and people who hire school premises. This duty is anticipatory, which means they have to plan ahead for disabled people who may want to come in the future. From December 2007 all schools had to produce a 'Disability Statement' which sets out how they are intending to move forward on implementing this duty. You can ask to see it at any educational provision you are considering for your child(ren).

Children which the system identifies as having special educational needs are entitled to the resources they need to participate in all the activities of the school from mealtime to examinations. Some resources are already 'delegated' to schools in their general school budget, and some are extra, obtainable through an 'SEN Statement'. Schools have a staged system of assessments to identify which level of support each child needs.

Find out what is happening in other schools and other local authorities. Gather together examples of good practice, of which there are many. Many of us found that we had to choose a mainstream school that was not our most local school on the basis that they had the leadership required to start the transformation to an inclusive school. Hopefully this will not always be the case as expertise and commitment spreads.

Get support. Everything becomes easier when you have at least one good 'ally' listening to you, coming with you to meetings, and helping you remain optimistic in the face of challenges and set backs. If possible find a whole group of people, including disabled adults who will help organise or campaign locally. Don't overlook professional allies, who, although it may be difficult for them to 'bite the hand that pays them' can put pressure on systems from the inside.

Support can also mean training, for yourself or for the services you are trying to influence. There are a number of national Training for Inclusion organisations which you could contact. (See back of book)

Build on what is working rather than concentrating on problem areas. If your child has made one friend at school, try to get to know their family. Ask the child round after school to play.

If all fails and you feel you must take your child out of a particular school, remember that the problem is not with you or your child, or with 'inclusion' or the 'mainstream' but that particular school and its unique set of personalities, policies and culture. Another school over the road may be completely different. Many young people labelled as having behaviour problems in one school, have flourished in another simply because the school has taken a different attitude towards him/her. The same is true for disabled young people and other minority groups.

Lastly, but most importantly, remember that you can always choose to be a leader. In fact you may not really have much choice. This can be a terrifying prospect for many who have not been raised to think of themselves this way. The circumstances of your life, and your love for your child(ren) may be asking you to develop and grow bigger than you ever thought possible. This, in the end, is a wonderful thing and you do not have to do it alone. There are many who have gone before you who will welcome you into the network. A leader is someone who helps people change, who has a vision of a better future and is willing to find out how to make it a reality. Rosaleen sets the challenge:

"Campaign with, alongside and on behalf of all disabled people. It has quite often been said that once you have a disabled person in the family, the whole family can then too experience disability. The moment you become frustrated by these experiences, you may wish to do something about it. If that is the case, join your local group of disabled people and become an activist. Disabled people have been fighting for change for over 100 years, and the Disabled People's Movement, is comprised of disabled people and our allies. Of course our allies are our family, our friends, our support workers, our peers, and any other like-minded individuals."
Rosaleen Moriarty-Simmonds

Disabled adults have been campaigning for inclusion in all areas of life ever since we started organising at all. Many of us have suffered deeply from the segregation policies of the past and we do not wish to see this happen to another generation of young people or to their families. It is true that we often face big struggles in the mainstream, but it is only by our presence that things have improved, and will continue to do so. Alan Tyne, a long time parent leader and campaigner for inclusive education speaks about the need for parents to join forces with disabled people:

"Parents and disabled people have always known in their hearts they must be the change they want to see in the world. But they need not do this alone. Wise alliances give us the courage and the strength to be and to do what we know we can. Wise allies do not bind our imagination, they free it so that we can see the world as it could be."
Alan Tyne

Aspirations

"The Disablement Resettlement Officer said I was unemployable because of my difficulty with writing/typing. They didn't know what to do with me. I believed him. I was disappointed. - no marriage, no kids, no job, no leaving home – no future it seemed was expected for me. But somewhere inside I still had hope I'd do something."
Edwina Macarthy

"What do you want to be?" is probably one of the most common questions adults ask children. We assume that a child will grow up and have a future which includes a useful role in the world. We also expect them to have friends, lovers, spouses and children.

If a child has a significant impairment all this changes. What you notice as a child is that no one talks about your future, or if they do, it is in a whispered, frightened "What will happen to her/him when I die?" sort of way. This lack of a positive picture leads you to have all sorts of fears, even a terror of growing up. Where are the stories and pictures of people like me living a good life? Where do they go? Maybe they all die? I remember that when I thought of myself aged about 25, all I could envision was a kind of blackness, a void. I knew my parents imagined I would always live with them until they popped their clogs, and then maybe they hoped I would move in with my sister. Both these scenarios seemed like hell to me, but I never told them.

Laureen talks about wanting a 'big life' despite the limited future others imagined for her:

"I never planned on a science career. I have cerebral palsy which affects my speech and muscle coordination movements. Throughout my education years, science was difficult to master and no one encouraged me to understand scientific theories, hypotheses, chemical reactions, and factual frameworks.

My deep curiosity about the world and my eagerness to make sense of my own life somehow seemed scientific in it of itself. My parents loved me and encouraged my independence, but I somehow felt their expectations, of what I would accomplish with my life, were small.

Witnessing the successes of others around me, I wanted more than to just get by. I wanted a big life and I wanted to make a difference in the world. When I was hired as an associate in a well-respected science organization that encouraged all students to pursue science, I realized that there is no limit to one's potential or how far one's mind can really go."
Laureen Summers

When I went to my segregated boarding school I met many other young disabled girls like me. I remember one of the first questions I was asked by a new friend as we sat in adjacent toilets was "Do you think you will ever get married?" I realised then that I was not alone in worrying about my future. I think everyone, young women in particular, have this fear lurking, especially with regard to the acceptability of our physical appearance, but nonetheless most people are held out the probability that it will be alright in the end. Not us.

Although the fantasy of falling in love and living happily ever after turns out not to be quite the reality for most people, we all need to grow up feeling that there are people outside of our own family or paid carers who would benefit from our company. We all need to be able to give and receive love:

"When I was first born the medical profession held out few expectations for my life. It may sound like a cliché but they actually said things like "she will remain a cabbage for the rest of her life, stuck lying on her back unable to do anything". How proud am I to have been able to prove them wrong.

Yes there was the initial round of hospitals and operations, years of rehabilitation and grappling to use artificial limbs. Having discarded those I was then liberated by the use of an electric wheelchair. A long battle to gain a good education, eventually lead to employment. A fantastic family and huge circle of friends lead to marriage and eventually motherhood.

113

So, do allow yourself to have expectations of your disabled child. From a very early age my parents soon came to realise that the so-called professionals got it completely wrong. My parents went on to have exactly the same wishes and expectations for me as they did for my two sisters."
Rosaleen Moriarty Simmonds

Laureen adds her own advice:

"It's quite a job for a parent to raise any child. A disability adds another dimension that challenges parents to learn a whole new set of care-giving techniques. Doctors, therapists and educators, who advise parents, often underestimate the true abilities of children with disabilities. We are taught to consider our peers, who have disabilities, as less able and less productive than a "normal" person. We are taught to be cautious and condescending toward anyone who appears dramatically different.

Parents have wonderful opportunities to contradict age-old assumptions. Advice from medical and educational professionals is well-meaning and parents can pick out the little gems of information to guide them. But parents must also follow their hearts, get to understand what their children want and need, and raise their own expectations about how much their child can really do. With technology and other appropriate accommodations for a disability, anything is possible. With good supports, there are truly no limits for anyone to develop their bodies and minds to the biggest extent possible."
Laureen Summers

Person Centred Planning Tools can help focus us, and our allies, on working systematically towards a positive future. A parent here commented on the feelings she had after being supported to create a PATH (Planning Alternative Tomorrows with Hope) for her daughter:

"I felt like I was reclaiming my daughter back. No one seemed to have any dreams, hopes, or ambitions for her – including me. The focus had always been on what she would never be able to do. I was always encouraged not to hope too much for her future in case I became disappointed. Or I was

told my expectations were too high and unrealistic. But every parent has great dreams for their child. Now, at last I can just do what comes natural to me as a mother" .*

* From 'All Our Children Belong', Exploring the Experiences of Black and Minority Ethnic Parents of Disabled Children' published by Parents for Inclusion 2004

Sex, Marriage and Babies

When I was a child it was assumed that I would remain single, untouched and unloved all my life. This was because my physical appearance was shaped by my genes, including my impairment, and also by the numerous fractures which I experienced as I was growing, or, more to the point, not growing. As a female my desirability in the marriage market was supposedly dependent on my looks, my figure and my ability to cook and clean up after a man. And of course the ability to have healthy babies. I was thought to be pretty deficient on all these counts.

I realised all this one lovely summer's day whilst gazing idly at some interesting cloud formations in the sky, when something went clang in my brain. Firstly, I suddenly realised that I was going to be disabled even as a 'grown up'. Up until then 'grown ups' seemed like a different species to 'children' – something we sort of metamorphose into at some distant time. As I had never seen anyone with my impairment as an adult, I thought I would somehow become able-bodied like all the other adults I knew. Apparently I was not alone in this delusion:

"I thought I would be able-bodied when I grew up. No one told me I wouldn't."
Edwina Macarthy

Secondly I could see that life was one big competition and I didn't have what it needed to win. Maybe it was hormones, but from that day onwards my life looked very different to me. I became very scared of my future. I felt like I was forever condemned to live in a fancy dress costume, unseen and unrecognised. The real me felt beautiful, sexy, loving and full of longing to express it all, but the messages I was receiving responded only to an image in other people's heads, not to me. These images came from the murky past of superstition, and eugenics, but I didn't know that then. I just knew that people thought I was weird, and I thought they were weird, dangerously so.

At that time I had never met a disabled adult who was living an 'ordinary life'. I had read no books, seen no films or television programmes or pictures to give me any kind of hope. There were no positive portrayals of disabled people, only the black and white charity ads aimed at evoking pity and guilt. Or books like Heidi and the Secret Garden where the disabled child character, turning out to be a hysteric, got up and walked. No one like me it seemed ever had a **life**.

On the streets I sometimes saw disabled adults in groups dressed like large children in big socks and sandals. I was horrified. I was aware that people viewed disabled people as always in need of care, never as people who could provide care to others. We were to be like perpetual children so the big socks and sandals made sense. The idea that we might one day become parents ourselves was a taboo subject. As most people still believed that any child we had would be more disabled than ourselves, and that we wouldn't be able to look after them, the very notion of our reproduction seemed to bring forth a kind of collective revulsion, something to be avoided at all costs.

Like many disabled people. I internalised a lot of these negative beliefs about myself during my teens and early twenties. I was very confused for a long time.

My family were not able to help me with these fears. They reinforced them. They told me that it was sad but true that no one would ever want me. They laughed or went silent when I spoke about having boyfriends or getting married, so I stopped talking about it. They could not understand why I wanted to wear fashionable clothes or make up which they thought looked ridiculous on me because of my diminutive size. They said that it was a shame I had such pretty hair. They did not do this out of malice. They were just voicing the prejudices of the time, but I needed something more. I needed allies.

With hindsight I can say a few things. Firstly, they were all wrong. There were, and are, plenty of people who could see past the 'differences' to the real me. I have had many friends, some lovers and a child for whom I took full responsibility. I have cared for many people in very effective ways, and all sorts of people have cared for me.

I have learned that non-disabled people are no happier than me, some much less so, and that the things which bring us true happiness are there in society for everyone, if they have the opportunity to find them. The problem for many disabled people is that our opportunities are restricted by over-protection, medical model policies which limit our horizons, prejudice and, worst of all, the internalised lack of confidence or sense of self worth which we may have absorbed from the attitudes around us.

My story is not unusual. To this day young disabled people struggle with these kind of negative ideas, but things are changing.

I now know many people with all kinds and levels of impairments who have deep connections with other people outside their family or an institution. Increasingly disabled people are building for themselves 'normal' lives, including sexual relationships with opposite or same sex partners, and are having or adopting children. People with learning difficulties are beginning to find support for their chosen relationships and with their parenting skills (although there is still a long way to go on this). Some disabled people choose to live with other disabled people, some choose non-disabled people. I know of several romances which have blossomed between disabled people and their paid 'personal assistants'. Some of us choose to live alone, but this does not have to mean that we are lonely. I was much lonelier when I was living amongst people who had no picture of who I was or shared any of my values.

I myself have not married yet, but then I am only 57.

I do know now that 'Happily Ever After' is not a reality for anyone.

What we all want from our parents is reassurance that we are OK as human beings, that we are likeable and have something to offer the world. We do not need to have our attention focussed on the hard things or the fears of adults, but on the hopeful things.

In terms of thinking about relationships in our adult lives, the most powerful thing to do is to meet people like us who have good lives – not necessarily the big stars or personalities like Stevie Wonder, Steven Hawkins or Tami Grey-Thompson who are exceptionally talented, but those people who have achieved 'ordinariness'. This is especially true for people with high level support needs, (i.e. they need a lot of one-to-one assistance in their daily lives), but who managed to leave the parental home (if they chose), found meaningful work (paid or unpaid), followed their own interests and hobbies, and who had a rich circle of relationships around them. You may have to do some research to find these role models, but a good start might be a local disabled –led organisation, a Centre for Independent Living, or a campaign group like the Alliance for Inclusive Education.

Meeting such people will also be the best support for you as a parent, to witness with your own eyes the new possibilities which are opening up in our evolving societies.

Assume all of life is going to happen to you child and help prepare them for it:

"Sex sadly is a taboo subject when used in the same sentence as disabled people. Society assumes that disabled people don't have sex, are not interested in sex, or are incapable of having sex.

Please realise that we are sexual beings, that disabled people have exactly the same wishes needs and desires for fulfilling relationships as non-disabled people. Don't assume that we will never have children, because many of us do.

However, the barriers that prevent us from enjoying relationships are - being able to access places where we can meet other people; people's negative attitudes towards and misconceptions about disabled people; and limited opportunities to experience sex, particularly if we rely on other people for our physical assistants and well-being.

I was always too embarrassed and uncomfortable about broaching the subject with my parents or expecting my parents to provide me with opportunities to have sex. Instead I had to rely on some very good

friends!"
Rosaleen Moriarty Simmonds

Teach all of your children the 'Facts of Life' and about Safe Sex, or make sure someone does. There are excellent resources which could help on video or picture books for young people with learning difficulties *(see Useful Resources at the back of this book)*.

Remember that there is a world out there full of human beings, the majority of whom are open, kind and keen to make real connections with others, including you and your child. If you feel your child is particularly vulnerable, make sure they have allies with them who will look out for them.

Thoughts about Meaningful Work

I have not met anyone who does not want to make a contribution to their families and communities. Very young people seem to be born with the notion that they should be able to put right any wrongs they see, and very elderly people greatly fear being viewed as people who are burdensome and no longer able to give. Many who wrote for this book appreciated the support they had been given to be able to work for a living:

"Like my parents my brother Phil and I grew up with a strong work ethic and to their credit we were bought up with the attitude that although we were disabled we would get jobs and contribute to society. I am grateful to them for this attitude because it has meant that we have both been financially independent and have had the satisfaction that work brings."
Mary Harrison

This desire is just as strong for people who have very high-level support needs such as Maresa:

"I want to give to the world. I watch, listen, and think. I am not distracted by endless things to do, as I can't do them. I need help to express myself, as I can't talk on my own, and if I didn't have physical help I would die. I can still give."
Maresa Mackeith

Yet, I am aware that the cold world of capitalism still has few places for those of us who do not match up to the current needs of the labour market.

At a conference for adults with learning difficulties I took part in a workshop on the notion of 'Person Centred Planning'. In this workshop we were asked to name a personal dream we had. A young man near me said, rather falteringly, that his big dream was to stack shelves in his local Sainsbury's. That was his dream and it seemed to him almost unobtainable. He was currently stuck in a day centre making bird boxes. He spoke about wanting a real job. He wanted to feel a useful part of his local community. He wanted to earn his own money because that would make him feel valued. He was painfully aware of the difference between being occupied at the day centre and being at work. Others in the circle said similar things.

It made me remember when I was in my early twenties and had left Art College in disillusionment. I knew I had something more meaningful to do with my life than design corn-flake boxes, but I was not sure what. I had thought, naively it turned out, that I would just get any old job whilst I worked out what my real 'work' was. I had passed my exams, I had done three years at Art College, what was the problem? Well apparently the problem was that I was a disabled person and too small to reach anything. After being turned down by employment agencies, not asked for interviews, sent to the Disablement Resettlement Officer and directed towards some kind of industrial rehabilitation scheme or the day centre which specialised in Arts and Crafts, I was in a state of shock. I realised that the world of work was even more rigid and inhuman than the education system which had also excluded me. Unless I could find a way to grow that extra two feet, I was considered unemployable. Unemployable. Unnecessary. Superfluous to need. Bringing things down to my level was not even a consideration. It was strange because it was not even work I wanted to do, but somehow the sense of rejection was enormous. I began to think that no one has the right to decide who should work and who shouldn't. To be able to share our personal gifts, talents, skills, thoughts, care – even love – for the benefit of others is a rational human need. It makes life meaningful. But I also began to realise, slowly, that there is a big difference between having a job in the capitalist sense, i.e. being productive within the economic system for the purposes of the owners, and real work, for the benefit of other human beings.

Now, after fifteen years of working towards an inclusive education system, and having some success, we are confronted anew by the problem of meaningful work. Young people with 'severe' impairments are finally taking their place alongside their brothers and sisters in ordinary schools, learning and teaching about being human. But at the end of school, what is on offer?

For some young adults who have been given enough support and a good dollop of luck, things are beginning to look hopeful. Joe Gault for example was born in 1981 and was one of the first children with learning difficulties to have a statement and go to a mainstream school with a learning support assistant. He went to a primary school in London and then Joe moved with his parents to Aberdeen in Scotland when he was twelve. Joe says:

"I am 22 now. I left college last year when I finished my NVQ in catering in 2003. This college is brilliant. I give them a 10 for inclusion.

I have four jobs. The first job is part time and I do this with my Dad teaching nurses about special education. I teach them that we are not different. They always give me the best evaluations. It is a fun job.

The second job is DJ'ing. My name is Joe90 and my business is called JK entertainment. I do Karaoke and discos at functions and DJ at pubs. I DJ any music except Gareth Gates and Will Young. The business was set up with my cousin Paul, but it is my business now. It is good. I want to carry on DJ'ing. It is my best interest.

My third job is recycling aluminium to keep the environment clean. I also recycle computer chips.

My fourth job is as vice-chair for People First. It is an organisation run by people with learning difficulties about speaking up. I have been a member since I was 16. We are all bosses. I like having someone to talk to. I feel quite confident."
Joe Gault*

However, for many young adults the future still has little to offer except endless segregated classes in FE Colleges, the Day Centres and the Bird Boxes, because little has fundamentally changed about how we value people. Being productive is everything.

* From 'Where Are They Now?' published by the Alliance for Inclusive Education 2005

If you think about any person when they are very young, they are busy. They are 'programmed' to fill every waking moment with exploration and learning. They are literally building their brains through gathering as many experiences as possible. To my mind this is their 'work' - to become themselves. Yet from the time of our birth, adults set about instilling in them their values, their agenda, their pace, their goals. Their own goals are thwarted many times a day. Their protests are called 'tantrums'. When they are tiny they do this with the health and social services monitoring, weighing, measuring, and testing for signs of 'trouble'. Soon, the education system takes over with its rigid timetables, curriculum, rules and values. By the time an average child in the rich world reaches her/his teens, she/he is expected to put in a 50 hour working week, at school and at home. They are not paid, have little choice of the content of their learning, the pace, style or manner of teaching. They are tested constantly and divided into successes and failures.

Interestingly, the work which is genuinely needed to provide for our real needs, such as growing food, building houses, driving buses, which could give those doing it great satisfaction and pride, is often considered very lowly, poorly paid and for the 'failures' within the system. They and the work they do, although everyone depends upon it, remain almost invisible.

Then there is the huge amount of work which people do voluntarily, but which is also absolutely vital for our survival, such as raising children, or caring for each other. This is what people do who are considered unemployed – doing 'nothing'. Then there are cultural workers - artists and musicians, writers and poets, dancers, actors and performers who help us to communicate our human values, help us to see our struggles in a wider context, link us together emotionally as well as exploring ideas.

There is a deeper vein still. That which some of would call our 'life's work'. This is where we put all our best thinking, our passions and dreams, our courage and commitment to make some unique contribution to humanity. For many of us this work has to remain 'underground', partly hidden from the mainstream world in which we have to survive. We often struggle to find the resources to carry out this work. It is probably where we stay connected with our childhood 'work' to become ourselves. They are probably part of the same thing. Only in this place can I see the possibility of inclusion. Those people most rejected by society because of their inability to fit the rigid mould of productivity have usually been given the least opportunity to fulfil their life's work – to become themselves. We have no idea really who they are. We see the terrible effects of their oppression, the patterns and injuries, and think it is them. We think it is evidence of their impairments or immorality. Those few people who have decided to be allies to those people, to help them become who they might be, have reported that it is the most exciting thing they can be doing. It seems that it cannot help but be a mutually beneficial thing.

So how do we create a society in which everyone is supported to do their life's work, and where would that lead us? This seems to me a question worth thinking about.

What Happens When You Die

Many of our parents were haunted by this fear as we grew up. Many of them are now dead, and we have survived to tell the tale.

Some of you may argue that those of us who are able to write for books and who have carved out good lives for ourselves are less 'disabled' than your children. This may be true, but in our parents day we were seen as 'too disabled' to manage without their care and protection because the services we now have didn't then exist.

The services we need have developed and grown because of pressure from families and disabled people. We now also have many allies thinking and fighting by our sides and legislation to protect our rights. This in turn has created a different, more inclusive culture in our societies.

I feel confident that it will become possible for people with even the highest level of need to live a life outside of an institution, with friends and purpose. Already there are experiments being made with individual Trusts managed by a Circle of Support as trustees. Equal Futures is one such project, currently based in Scotland:

"For those of us who have a relative with a disability, one of the most pressing questions we face is "What will happen to my loved one when I am no longer here?" No matter how much money is left to an individual, how well a will is written or how good the current support services are, we will never have peace of mind unless we know that there are other people who love and care for our relative after we have gone.

Equal Futures was created to support families to answer this question. We build lifelong Circles of Support around individuals and their families. These circles consist of family, friends neighbours, previous support staff, colleagues etc, in other words a group of people who care for the person at the centre and are passionate about ensuring a good life for them.

We build circles by recruiting and matching a paid facilitator to a family.

Using a range of Person Centred Planning tools the facilitator will look at what people and places creates energy, enthusiasm and excitement for the individual, and who is already involved in their life. People will then be invited to become circle members. The circles meet regularly; where they dream and make goals, look at what's working well and what the focus person needs the support of the circle to accomplish. The meetings are not formal events and sometimes are purely social with different circles getting together.

We support families to plan for the future by completing a Future Planning Consultation and a family profile. These will help you begin to look at the hopes and dreams of your loved one, and just as importantly the fears and nightmares and what practical steps you have already taken and what gaps you have to fill. We hold regular information sessions hosted by a range of professionals on Wills and Trusts, Powers of Attorney and Guardianship, Ownership Options and Financial Planning.

Families are in control of the circles at all times. Much of the membership costs pay directly for the facilitators' hours and the network co-ordinators are in regular contact with everyone involved providing support and guidance.
Equal Futures 2008

Their role is not only to safeguard the person's finances, but also their lifestyle and wellbeing. With the advent of Direct Payments, Personal Budgets, and greater inclusion educationally and socially, it seems inevitable that person-centred and user led services such as Equal Futures will spread throughout the UK, if not the world. It is our hope that a vibrant network of properly funded and stable All Age Centres for Independent Living will house these services in every Local Authority. It must be remembered that not all disabled people do have loving and supportive parents, even as young people, so alternative ways of supporting them, based on their human rights, have to be found.

Celebrating Short Lives

A Tribute to Nihal Armstrong

You have left us with many memories
We miss you every day
Sometimes we think of you
Not more than today
You will never be forgotten
In our hearts you are and there you'll stay
You were a really good friend
And this we will never forget . . . .
I'm sure he loved his family most of all
But shared himself with all who called
And no prejudice nor hate
But accepted life just on his faith
His life was short but full of love
For family, friends and god above
So short a time with us it seems
No time to really fill his dreams
This is written to him in honour
For all that we did share
I just want him to know
How much we really did care.

Syeda Momena Aktar from 11Y,
Camden Community School, London, published in 'Inclusion Now', Issue 5

No child is born with a guaranteed time on earth, but it is a fact that some impairments do shorten a person's life. As a disabled person I have said goodbye to many childhood friends, comrades and lovers, because their physical or emotional strength gave out. Even at the point of death the medical and social models have effect. I have witnessed both.

In my special school, during the three years I was there, seven young disabled people died. They all died away from school, in hospital, one in a road accident. My memory is that the deaths were announced by the head teacher in morning assembly with no preparation or warning for us however close we had been. A prayer was prayed. A hymn was sung and that was the end of it. There was usually very little emotional reaction on our part, because we had gone numb. I do not recall any of the children being spoken about again by the adults. We were left to cope as best we could. Questions were rarely answered because of 'confidentiality'. I am still grieving for some of these children forty years later.

In my daughter's mainstream secondary school, in the seven years she was there, two children died. One died in an accident in the school playground, the other died of a form of muscular dystrophy in her early teens. Both deaths were responded to in similar ways – the whole school was told, a leaflet was written and printed for all the parents in the school explaining what had happened, some ways in which their children may be affected, and ways in which their parents could support them. Bereavement counsellors were hired and brought into school. Many opportunities to ask questions were created during the following days. The families of the dead children were encouraged and supported to invite their child's friends to the funerals. The Head Teacher went to visit the families at home and spoke at the funerals along with other teachers and support staff.

In the school, in the case of the boy who had died in the playground, and acknowledging the large extended family who had flown into England from the West Indies to attend the funeral, the Head Teacher organised a party to help celebrate the boy's life whilst all the relatives were still in the country. For the girl who died a whole school memorial celebration was organised. Both children were allocated a whole wall inside the school for people to put up their memories, photos, poems and pictures, and these walls were maintained and visible for over a year. There are over 1200 pupils in the school and every one was made perhaps sadder, but certainly richer by the school experience of loss. They learned an important lesson in the value of every human life. No one said 'it's all for the best' or 'their suffering is over now' or any such nonsensical platitudes. They spoke instead of the gifts that had been given them by their friends and schoolmates and eased the parents' grief by sharing it. This to me was a true model of inclusion.

Remember You are Loved

Parents love their children and children love their parents. Most of us are very forgiving of the shortcomings of our parents and very aware of the struggle they had to bring us up without enough information, support or appreciation. Many people who wrote for this book were keen to make sure that their parents were not blamed for the difficulties the world had created.

You do not have to be perfect, you did not fail us. You have given us the gift of life and we are making the most of it:

"My wonderful Dad, the best father in the world. Every child with a disability should come with one as standard and made-to-measure like my father."
Sapna Ramnani

"I think that they (my parents) did their best but without support it was very difficult for them. My parents were very good at pooling their resources to give me a good life. I would like to say that my parents did the best they could for me."
Larry O'Bryan

"I always felt loved by my parents. I was always told I was beautiful and that someone would love me. That I'd have lots of boyfriends. There was 'someone there for everyone'. They also pushed me to do things which were about my intellectual needs. I think they always did the right thing by me. They coped well when there was no support."
Baroness Jane Campbell

"The word love has many different meanings, but the context I'm thinking about is unconditional love. I know that no matter how tired my parents were, no matter how hard things got, no matter how financially they may have struggled, their love for me was unconditional and absolute.

In return, my love, gratitude and respect for them, and my family, was supreme and has never faltered. I am in the privileged position of being able to tell them how much I love them. But bearing in mind the fact that

communication between people is made up of many facets and speech only accounts for 10% of the way we communicate with others, there are lots of ways that we can show our disabled children how much we love them and millions of ways for them to reciprocate."
Rosaleen Moriarty Simmons

"During my childhood, with all the hardships my parents, brother and myself faced, I never doubted that we were loved. My parents were both very loving and affectionate people and I have many happy memories of childhood although these were always short lived as return to boarding school was always an inevitable end to the short bouts of happiness. As an adult now in my fifties I realise just what a struggle my parents had to bring us up. I think human beings can endure any hardships in childhood so long as they believe they are loved."
Mary Harrison

"It is often the parent who has fought for the inclusion of their child and has been able to hold up high expectations for their success. They are the ones who have led the way to success for all children with disabilities to grow up and choose a lifestyle that is most rewarding and celebratory of themselves."
Laureen Summers.

"I would never have believed when I was a child that one day I would get an MBE and be a managing director of an organisation (The Quality Company). I feel like I am blessed. Many of my friends are still in Day Centres worried about who will look after them when their parents die. My Mum is getting older now and I have to look after her. She looked after us all as best she could. I would like to thank her for believing in my rights as a person with learning difficulties."
Jackie Downer MBE

"Although my parents are no longer here, I want to raise a toast to them and say "Thank you for believing, encouraging, supporting, guiding and loving me; for letting me make mistakes; for being there to pick up the pieces; for sharing your wisdom – and letting me go into the world to follow my own path."
Wilma Laurie

Useful Books and Magazines

All My Life's a Circle –
Using the Tools: Circles, MAPs and PATH
M. Falvey, M. Forest, J. Pearpoint and R. Rosenberg,
Available from Inclusive Solutions and Inclusion Press
The widely popular, user-friendly introduction to these useful and exciting tools for change.

Creating Circles of Friends
Colin Newton & Derek Wilson,
Published by Inclusive solutions.
A must for anyone interested in building friendships and relationships around those vulnerable or challenging through reason of disability or emotional need.

Families Leading Planning
Alison Short & Helen Sanderson with Margaret Cook
Available from Inclusive Solutions
A pack specifically designed for family members to take the lead planning with or for a person who has learning difficulties. It is based on a particular form of person-centred planning called 'Essential Lifestyle Planning'.

Freaks, Geeks and Asperger Syndrome
A User Guide to Adolescence
Luke Jackson
Published by Jessica Kingsley Publishers
Written by a thirteen year old boy with the diagnosis of Asperger Syndrome, this book is aimed at other young people like himself who know they are 'different'. It is very illuminating for all who read it.

Four Fingers and Thirteen Toes
Rosaleen Moriarty Simmonds
ISBN No 0954888324
Can be purchased through most good high street book stores, through

major online book retailers such as www.amazon.co.uk and directly from Rosaleen by e-mailing: rms-bookorders@dsl.pipex.com

Four Fingers and Thirteen Toes charts Rosie's birth into an Irish immigrant family, her early years filled with long periods of hospitalisation and treatment; her education, employment and relationships; and onto true fulfilment of a lifetime's desire to be independent...

...It continues with the history and assessment of how the so called "wonder drug" of the 1960s, thought to be banished after the tragedy unfolded, is still being used in the treatment of various conditions and illnesses. It examines why pharmaceutical companies are eager for it to be re-licensed and includes Rosie's honest perspective of the drug.

Inclusion Now
Subscriptions from the Alliance for Inclusive Education (free to members)
A unique termly magazine by and for parents, teachers, disabled people and all who consider themselves part of the UK inclusion movement.

Incurably Human
Micheline Mason
Published by Inclusive Solutions
Here you can learn about the history of segregation, the rise of the disability movement and the story of how parents, disabled people and professionals are working together to transform the education system, and the implication of such change for our future societies.

Listening to Children
Patty Wipfler
Published by Hand in Hand,
P.O. Box 1279, Palo Alto, CA 94302,
www.handinhandparenting.org
Written for parents and caregivers, it explains in down-to-earth terms what children want and need from the people who love them. You'll learn why children express their feelings so fully, and how to help them with their difficulties. You'll learn how your child's mind works, and how listening to your child allows the two of you to work together to relieve you

child's fears, frustrations, and anger. Winner of the NAPPA Gold award in 2006. The seven booklets include: **How Children's Emotions Work, Special Time, Playlistening, Crying, Tantrums and Indignation, Healing Children's Fears, and Reaching For Your Angry Child.** *Also -*

Listening Partnerships for Parents
Patty Wipfler

A practical guide to listening parent-to-parent. Hand in Hand has found that parents who set up listening partnerships make steady gains in their ability to be pleased with themselves and with their children. This booklet describes how the listening process works to empower parents and to relieve the stresses in our lives. How to set up a listening partnership, how to listen, how to use a listener, and how to begin working on key issues for parents are discussed in depth.

All publications sold via the Internet in both hard copy and PDF formats.

Snapshots of Possibility –
Shining Examples of Inclusion
Compiled by Jackie Dearden
The Alliance for Inclusive Education

Examples of good practice in inclusive education drawn from nurseries, schools and colleges throughout the UK.

The Essential family Guide
How to Help your Family Member be in Control
Caroline Tomlinson
In Control Publications,
4 Swan Courtyard, Coventry Road, Birmingham B26 1BU

A guide to getting and using personal budgets as part of the In Control Project (see useful organisations and websites). Most appropriate for parents of disabled adults.

Where Are They Now?
Travelling the Road to Inclusion
Compiled by Emily Peasgood and Wendy Greenwell
The Alliance for Inclusive Education

Inspiring Interviews with sixteen young disabled people whose parents had joined the Alliance in order find support in their struggles for properly supported mainstream education. They speak of their lives as young adults and their hopes for the future.

Words Unspoken
Self published
Available from Inclusive Solutions
The first UK collection of writings from seven young users of Facilitated Communication.

You're Going to Love This Kid
Paula Kluth
Available from Inclusive Solutions
Allows the lived experience of people with autism to teach us how to create inclusive classrooms which work. Aimed at teachers, but of great relevance to parents and all who wish to think better about young people with autism.

Useful Organisations

Action for Kids
Ability House, 15a Tottenham Lane, Hornsey, London N8 9DJ
Tel: 0208 347 3482 Helpline: 0845 300 0273
www.actionforkids.org.uk
Provides disabled children and young people up to the age of 26 with mobility equipment. Most is supplied on a long-term loan scheme which covers maintenance and servicing.

The Alliance for Inclusive Education
336 Brixton Road, London SW9 7AA
Tel: 020 7737 6030
www.allfie.org.uk
A national membership organisation, led by disabled people, helps organise parents, teachers and allies to promote and campaign for an entitlement to good quality inclusive education for all young people. Allfie's current projects include youth-led forums for young people in danger of social exclusion, and 'Heading for Inclusion', a group of Head Teachers and other senior school managers who believe in the principles and practice of inclusive education.
The Alliance has designed a training pack called 'The Inclusion Assistant' for those who support young people with high-level support needs in mainstream schools. They also deliver a 'Training the Trainers' course on its use in collaboration with the Institute for Education. They have many publications including the termly magazine 'Inclusion Now' produced in collaboration with Parents for Inclusion and Disability Equality in Education.

Candle
48 Station Road, Holywell Green, HX4 9HW
Tel: 01422 835 494
www.contactcandle.co.uk
If you want to know more about Facilitated Communication or forms of augmentative technology for people who cannot communicate using their voice, here is a good place to start.

Danda

Developmental Adult Neuro-Diversity Association
46 Westbere Road, London NW2 3RU
Tel: 0207 435 7891
www.danda.org.uk
A user-led group of people with Dyspraxia, Asperger Syndrome, AD(H)D, Tourettes Syndrome, and association conditions such as Dyslexia and Discalcula. Their mission is to: "See that adults with developmental neuro-diversity reach their full potential and play a full role in society". A great source of information and role models for parents and young people.

The Disability Alliance

Universal House, 88-94 Wentworth Street, London E1 7SA
Tel: (voice and minicom) 0207 247 8776
www.disabilityalliance.org
An important source of information about allowances, benefits, tax credits and grants for disabled people. Publishes 'Don't Miss Out', A Guide to Benefits and Services for Disabled Children and their Families' including a chapter on help for 'carers'.

Disability Equality in Education

Unit GL, 436 Essex Road, London N1 3QP
Tel: 0207 359 2855
www.diseed.org.uk
Delivers high quality training, by disabled DET Trainers, to nurseries, schools and other relevant services on disability equality and inclusion for disabled young people, including the implementation of the Disability Discrimination Act within the educations system.
Has an excellent online bookstore including many books for children with a disability equality ethos.

Disabled Parents Network

81 Melton Road, West Bridgford, Nottingham, NG2 8EN
Tel: 0870 241 0450
www.disabledparentsnetwork.org.uk

DPN is a national organisation of and for disabled people who are, or hope to become, parents, plus their families, friends and supporters. They offer a range of support including a national helpline, and publish a quarterly newsletter.

Equal Futures
54 Manor Place, Edinburgh, EH3 7EH
Tel: 0131 226 5454
www.equalfutures.org.uk
Sets up lifelong circles of support around individuals and their families using person centred planning tools. Although currently limited to the central belt of Scotland, they are trailblazing new and creative alternatives to institutionalisation. Anyone cam subscribe to their newsletter or ask for their support to start a similar venture in your own area.

The Family Fund
Unit 4, Alpha Court, Monks Cross Drive, Huntingdon, York YO32 9WN
Tel: 0845 130 45 42
Tex phone 01904 658 085
www.familyfund.org.uk
The Family Fund "Champions an inclusive society where families with severely disabled children (up to the age of sixteen) can have choices and opportunities to enjoy an ordinary life"
They are a Government sponsored Charity and give grants for household equipment such as freezers, computers and washing machines as well as help with holidays and outings.

HEYA Collective Ltd
Helping Empower Youth Activism
c/o 34a Dafforne Road, Tooting, London SW17 8TZ
Tel: 07943 263 478
"HEYA is a youth lead collective. Our aim is to create a vast network of young activists and community leaders passionate about progressive social change, equipped with the tools necessary to insure that the movement becomes fully inclusive.
Our job is to create an environment where young people feel completely

welcome. There are many ways to achieve this, workshops, support groups, interactive forums all of which will need to tackle racism, homophobia, sexism, disability and class oppression head on".

HEYA trainers are available to run young people's events around the UK and abroad.

Inclusive Solutions

49 Northcliffe Avenue, Nottingham, NG3 6DA

Queries: 01473 437 590

www.inclusive-solutions.com

Set up by two senior educational psychologists committed to developing good practice around inclusive education and community living for young people with impairments or emotional and behavioural difficulties. They offer training for service providers all over the UK, and some support for families. They have an excellent website with a well-stocked online store of books and other resources.

National Centre for Independent Living

4th Floor, Hampton House, Albert Embankment, London SE1 7TJ

Tel: 0207 587 1663

www.ncil.org.uk

A National organisation giving information and advice on Direct Payments, Individual Budgets, including a DVD – Direct Payments A Beginners Guide. They will have information about local support groups and centres for independent living (CILs).

Parents for Inclusion

Room 1, Winchester House, Kennington Park Business Centre, Cranmer Road, London SW9 6EJ

Tel: 0207 735 7735

www.parentsforinclusion.org

A national organisation led by parents of disabled children, working in partnership with disabled adults, promoting the social model of disability to parents, allies and service providers.

PI runs a national helpline for parents and others on all issues related to inclusive education; school – based inclusion groups for parents; Planning

Positive Futures, a training course for parents introducing them to the medical/social model and helping them to become more powerful allies to their children; The Training Pathway, an eighteen month accredited course for parents wishing to become trainers, facilitators and to generally develop their leadership potential in the area of inclusion; the Welcome Project, a pack and associated training for people working with parents of new-born or newly diagnosed young disabled people to help counteract negativity and set them on the path to an inclusive life.

People First (Self-Advocacy)
Hampton House, 4th Floor, 20 Albert Embankment, London SE1 7TJ
Tel: 0207 820 6655
www.peoplefirstltd.com
An organisation run by and for people who have the label of 'learning difficulty'. They raise awareness of and campaign for the rights of people with learning difficulties and support self-advocacy groups across the country.

RADAR (Royal association for Disability and Rehabilitation)
12 City Forum, 250 City Road, London EC1V 8AF
Tel: 0207 250 3222 Minicom: 0207 250 4119
www.radar.org.uk
The largest general information organisation in the UK, and, most importantly, the source of the keys to all those locked toilets!

Whizz Kidz
Elliot House, 10 -12 Allington Street, London SW1E 5EH
Te;: 0207 233 6600
www.whizz-Kidz.org.uk
"Whizz Kidz is a charity all about giving disabled children the chance to lead a more independent life. Our services meet their mobility needs and ensure they get the right mobility equipment, advice and training at the right time".